Cambridge English

for Movers

Student's Book
Third edition

Anne Robinson
Karen Saxby

Cambridge University Press
www.cambridge.org/elt

Cambridge English Language Assessment
www.cambridgeenglish.org

Information on this title: www.cambridge.org/9781107444782

© Cambridge University Press 2015

First published 2006
Second edition 2010
Third edition 2015
5th printing 2015

Printed in Italy by Rotolito Lombarda S.p.A.

A catalogue record for this publication is available from the British Library

ISBN 978-1107-44478-2 Student's Book with audio and online activities
ISBN 978-1107-44480-5 Teacher's Book with audio
ISBN 978-1107-44481-2 Class Audio CD
ISBN 978-1107-48404-7 Presentation Plus DVD-ROM

Download the audio at www.cambridge.org/funfor

The authors and publishers would like to thank the ELT professionals who commented on the material at different stages of its development:

The authors are grateful to: Niki Donnelly of Cambridge University Press

Anne Robinson would like to give special thanks to Adam Evans and her parents Margaret and Jim and to many many teachers and students who have inspired her along the way. Special thanks to Cristina and Victoria for their help, patience and enthusiasm. And in memory of her brother Dave.

Karen Saxby would like to give special thanks to everyone she has worked with at Cambridge Assessment since the birth of YLE! She would particularly like to mention Frances, Felicity and Ann Kelly. She would also like to acknowledge the enthusiasm of all the teachers she has met through her work in this field. And lastly, Karen would like to say a big thank you to her sons, Tom and William, for bringing constant FUN and creative thinking to her life and work.

Editorial work by Bridget Kelly

Cover design by Crush Creative

Book design and page make-up by emc design Ltd

The authors and publishers are grateful to the following illustrators:
Laetitia Aynié (Sylvie Poggio Artists Agency) pp. 6 (T), 7 (BL), 17 (C), 19, 29 (T), 30 (BL), 31 (B), 33 (T), 39 (T), 48, 58 (B), 62 (C), 63 (T), 67 (B), 77 (B), 81 (C), 82 (T), 90 (T), 92, 100 (T); Johanna A Boccardo (Sylvie Poggio Artists Agency) pp. 36 (B), 52, 53 (CR), 68 (TR); Nina de Polonia (Advocate Art) pp. 11 (T), 18 (C), 21 (C), 24 (TL), 27 (B), 40, 60 (B), 69 (C), 104; Bridget Dowty (Graham-Cameron Illustration) pp. 23 (CL), 26 (T), 39 (B), 74 (T); Andy Elkerton (Sylvie Poggio Artists Agency) pp. 8 (T), 9 (T), 21 (B), 28 (C), 51 (T), 58 (T), 73 (T), 89 (B), 109, 110; Chris Embleton-Hall (Advocate Art) pp. 28 (T), 46 (T); Brett Hudson (Graham-Cameron Illustration) pp. 29 (BR), 31 (C), 38 (1, 2, 5, 6, 8), 55, 61 (C), 70 (B), 71, 73 (C), 76 (T), 83 (B), 94 (T); Nigel Kitching (Sylvie Poggio Artists Agency) pp. 8 (C), 12, 17 (T), 42, 43, 62 (T), 64, 106 (BR), 108; Andrew Painter (Sylvie Poggio Artists Agency) pp. 10 (C), 11 (B), 15 (C), 25 (T), 35, 37 (T), 50 (C), 51 (B), 53 (BR), 63 (B), 66 (C), 68 (B), 78, 79 (T), 84, 85, 88 (B), 93 (B), 98 (TR), 102 (B), 103 (B), 112 (B), 114 (T), 115; Jamie Pogue (The Bright Agency) pp. 9 (B), 20, 24 (B), 36 (T), 45, 47, 59 (C), 60 (T), 61 (BR), 111, 112 (T); Andre?s Ricci (The Organisation) pp. 6 (B), 13, 16 (B), 23 (BR), 32 (T), 34, 38 (3, 4, 7), 41 (BR), 53 (T), 76 (B), 77 (T), 79 (B), 83 (T), 88 (T), 97, 101, 103 (T); Anthony Rule pp. 5, 7 (BR), 11 (BC), 18 (TR), 25 (B), 28 (TR), 31 (BR), 33 (BR), 36 (TR), 37 (BR), 44 (TR), 49 (CR), 50 (TR), 59 (TR), 66 (TR), 69 (BR), 74 (TR), 79 (BR), 85 (BR), 87 (BR), 88 (TR), 96 (TR), 104 (T); Pip Sampson pp. 15 (T), 18 (BR), 22, 23 (CR), 30 (T), 31 (T), 38 (T), 56, 57, 62 (B), 72, 73 (B), 82 (B), 90 (B), 94 (B), 95, 96 (C), 102 (TR), 106 (TR), 107; Melanie Sharp (Sylvie Poggio Artists Agency) pp. 10 (TR), 16 (T), 17 (B), 41 (T), 54, 67 (T), 81 (B), 86, 98 (C), 99, 105, 113, 114; Emily Skinner p. 93 (T); Jo Taylor (Sylvie Poggio Artists Agency) pp. 25, 74 (B), 75, 89 (T), 100 (BR); Sarah Wimperis (Graham-Cameron Illustration) pp. 46 (BL), 91; Sue Woollatt pp. 14, 26 (B), 27 (T), 44 (C), 70 (T), 80, 87.

The authors and publishers acknowledge the following sources of copyright material and are grateful for the permissions granted. While every effort has been made, it has not always been possible to identify the sources of all the material used, or to trace all copyright holders. If any omissions are brought to our notice, we will be happy to include the appropriate acknowledgements on reprinting.

Sound recordings by dsound Recording Studios, London

Contents

1 Watch us! We're moving!

Ⓐ ▶ Listen and draw lines.

May   Kim   Tom   Sue   Dan

Ann   Pat   Jack   Jill   Sam

....

Ⓑ Read and write names.

Watch us! We're moving!

...Jack...'s good at jumping. He's really great!

And look! ....'s hopping on square number 8!

.............'s skating now! She's going round and round.

And watch .... skipping in our new playground.

.............'s good at dancing! One, two, three.

And there's .... He's funny! He's climbing our tree!

.............'s very good at running. He runs all day!

But .... likes walking (and talking) with her best friend, ...

Jump, hop, skate, skip,

dance, climb or run.

We all love moving and having lots of fun!

Ⓒ Listen and draw four things in picture A.

D **Find the letters to spell the missing moving word!**

_ _ _ _ b _ _ _

E **Look at picture A and read. Write yes or no.**

Examples:	You can see a tree.	...yes...
	A boy is sitting on the box.	...no...
1	A blue bird is sitting on the bike.	....
2	Someone is playing basketball.	....
3	One person is holding a round balloon.	....
4	The teacher is wearing a pair of red trousers.	....
5	A boy is kicking a white football.	....
6	Three children are standing in a circle.	....

F **About you! Say and write answers.**

Who do you play with in your playground?   I play with ....

Is your playground big or small?   It's ....

What are you good at?   I'm good at ....

Tell me about your friend.

What's your friend's name?   My friend's name is ....

How old is your friend?   My friend is ....

What's your friend good at?

....

2 'Animals, animals ...'

A Say then write the animals.

1	2	3	4 ....
5	6	7	8 ....
9	10	11	12 ....

B Which parts of a crocodile can you see in pictures 1–4?

its ....   its ....   its ....   its .... and its ....

C How much do you know about crocodiles? Write yes or no.

1 Do crocodiles only live in rivers? ....
2 Do crocodiles open their eyes when they are swimming? ....
3 Can crocodiles swim and walk? ....
4 Do crocodiles have lots of teeth? ....
5 Do crocodiles eat birds? ....
6 Is it safe to go swimming with a crocodile? ....
7 Is a baby crocodile inside its egg for 20 weeks? ....

Are your answers right? Read about crocodiles on page 106.

D Read and write the animal names.

1 It has a tail and it likes catching mice. It sounds like 'hat'. ....*cat*............
2 It's always hungry and it has a little beard. It sounds like 'boat'. ....
3 It's very small and it eats cheese. It sounds like 'house'. ....
4 It's green and it jumps very well. It sounds like 'dog'. ....
5 It eats grass. It sounds like 'now'. ....
6 It sings and sometimes lives in a cage. It sounds like 'word'. ....
7 It lives in the sea. I'm frightened of it! It sounds like 'park'. ....
8 It has no legs and makes a noise like 'sssss'. It sounds like 'cake'. ....
9 It's really big and it swims in the sea. It sounds like 'tail'. ....
10 It flies at night. It sounds like 'Pat'. ....

E ▶ Listen and write.

Peter's day at the zoo

Example	Name of zoo:	.......*World*....... Zoo
1	Who with:	....
2	Can see:	.... monkeys
3	Favourite animals:	....
4	Can ride on:	a ....
5	Wants to buy:	a ....

F Now play the game! It sounds like ... .

3 Fun at the farm

A What's on the farm?

a cloud

a field

a truck

a roof

a chicken

a rabbit

a duck

a kitten

B Read and then complete the sentences. Write one word.

Let's go to Mrs Plant's farm!

On Saturday afternoons, ... and his sister, ... ,
go to help Mrs Plant on her farm. They carry potatoes and give the animals
their food. The children ride there on their bikes because it is near their
home. Mrs Plant has two new animals on the farm now! She's got a kitten
called Sunny and a puppy called Sausage! They're both really sweet.

1   The children go to the farm every ....Saturday.... afternoon.
2   Mrs .... lives on the farm.
3   The children .... Mrs Plant's potatoes for her.
4   The children ride their .... to the farm.
5   Mrs Plant's kitten is called ....
6   The pets on the farm are very ....

C ▶ Listen and colour.

D Say which picture is different and why.

1

2

3

4

E Which animals live in these places?
Write their names.

Which three animals are you
frightened of? ....

....

Which are your three favourite
animals? ....

....

Which animal would you like
to be?
I'd like to be a ....!

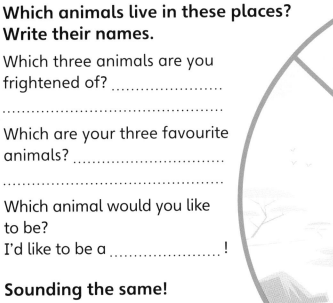

F Sounding the same!

there

they're

their

G Do the animal project!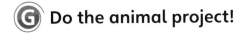

11

4 'Your hair looks great!'

A Write the answers to the questions.

1 What colour's her hair?

2 What's this?

3 What kind of hair has he got?

4 What's this?

5 Is her hair long or short?

6 What kind of hair has she got?

B Talk about your hair.

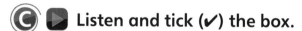

| I've got | long | straight | blonde   fair   red   brown | hair. |
| I have | ....short....... | .... | black   grey/gray   white | |

C ▶ Listen and tick (✔) the box.

1 Which girl is Kim?

A ☐   B ☐   C ☐

2 Which man is Mr Scarf?

A ☐   B ☐   C ☐

3 Which person is Jim's cousin?

A ☐   B ☐   C ☐

4 Which boy is Paul's friend?

A ☐   B ☐   C ☐

D **Read about Alex. Write 1, 2 or 3 words to complete the sentences.**

Change Alex's face for the film.

Alex Top is really famous because he's a film star. The name of his seventh film is *What's that noise?* Alex is making it now. In this film, his body and face look very different. Alex is an alien!

Before filming, Alex puts on his orange alien suit and then sits down in front of a big mirror. Then Jane starts changing his face. First, she paints it green. Then someone paints black lines on his face and changes the colour of his eyes.

A third person, called Ben, adds a moustache and beard to Alex's face and a fourth person changes his short, straight blonde hair to long, curly purple hair!

Then Alex can start filming. 'Your face looks really ugly now!' everyone says. Alex looks in the mirror again and laughs. 'Great!' he says, 'Thank you!'

Examples   Alex Top is a ....*famous*........ film star.

His seventh film is called ....*What's that noise?*....

1   In Alex's new film, his .... and body look very different.
2   Alex isn't a person from our world. He's an ....!
3   Alex sits down in front of a .... in his orange clothes.
4   A woman makes Alex's face green. Her name is ....
5   Another person paints some .... on his face, too.
6   Ben puts two things on Alex's face – a ....
7   Alex has to have ...., curly and purple hair in this film.
8   Everyone thinks Alex's face looks very ....!
9   When Alex looks at his face he .... and then says 'Thank you!'

E **Play the game. Find the person.**

F **She looks surprised!**

13

5 'The woman in the red dress'

A Find the words for the pictures and write them on the lines.

1

........scarf........

s	c	a	r	f	g	r	t	w
w	o	s	s	s	l	s	s	h
e	a	h	o	h	a	k	h	l
a	t	i	c	o	s	i	i	d
t	b	r	k	e	s	r	r	r
e	a	t	s	s	e	t	t	e
r	g	h	a	t	s	e	i	s
y	t	r	o	u	s	e	r	s

8

....

2

....

7

....

3

....

4

....

5

....

6
....

B Find the words in the box for five more things you wear.

C Choose the correct words from A or B. Write them on the lines.

1   In cold weather, you can wear this round your neck.   a ....scarf........
2   This is like a very long jacket which you can wear outside.   a ....
3   You can wear these on your feet inside your shoes.   ....
4   People can put their things into this and then carry it.   a ....
5   A pair of these can help some people to read a book.   ....

D Say the words.

Yes, I can swim!

No, I can't fly!

14

E Write the words from A and B in the table.

top half	bottom half	top and bottom half
scarf	a pair of socks	coat

F ▶ Listen and draw lines.

Ann   Fred   John   Peter

Lucy   Jane   Tom

G Look at the picture and read. Write **yes** or **no**.

Examples   Two children are riding bikes in this park.   ...yes...
            The monster is sitting behind two small trees.   ...no...

1   A man with a beard is reading a funny book.   ....

2   Three people are eating chocolate ice creams.   ....

3   The black and white football is on the ground.   ....

4   There is a small blue and white chair next to the green seat.   ....

5   The girl in the purple skirt has got straight black hair.   ....

6   Only one boy is wearing a pair of glasses.   ....

H Ask and answer questions.

Let's talk about the clothes you wear!

6 'My neck, my shoulders'

A **How many?**

hands	26
eyes	....
legs	....
ears	....
backs	....
mouths	....
wings	....

B **Longer than, shorter than? Cross out the wrong word.**

The monsters' legs are *longer / shorter* than the children's legs.

The children's hair is *longer / shorter* than the monster's hair.

The monsters' mouths are *bigger / smaller* than the children's mouths.

The children's heads are *bigger / smaller* than the monsters' heads.

The man is *shorter / taller* and *younger / older* than everyone!

C **My neck, my shoulders and my stomach!**

Listen and point.

my neck

my shoulder

my stomach

D **Find the correct words and write them on the lines.**

Example   This is between your eyes and your mouth.   ....nose.........

1   After your dinner, your food is inside this.   ....

2   This is hair on a man's face. It's under his mouth.   ....

3   You stand on these. They are at the end of your legs.   ....

4   These are white and you have lots in your mouth.   ....

5   You have two of these and you listen with them.   ....

6   This is under your head and above your shoulders.   ....

searsoteethlnosehfeeteneckrstomachubeardd

The mystery word is ....

E **Put the balls in the correct net!**

1   The monsters' arms are very short.

2   One of the monsters is holding a cup.

3   There's a flower on one monster's stomach.

4   The robot that's outside the house is laughing.

5   You can see a monster on the round roof.

6   The monster next to the door is wearing a pair of shoes.

F **The monsters go home to the moon! Listen and colour.**

G **Play the game! Answer with your body.**

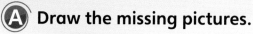

A Draw the missing pictures.

a coat

clouds

the wind

a kangaroo

rain

bats

a scarf

the moon

B Choose the correct words and write them on the lines.

Example   This is longer than a jacket and you wear it outside.   *a coat*

1   You can see this and the stars above you at night.   ....

2   These only fly at night and some people are afraid of them.   ....

3   When you walk in this weather, your clothes get wet!   ....

4   This animal can hop and it lives in a hot, sunny, country.   ....

5   It's a good idea to wear this round your neck on colder days.   ....

6   These are white or grey and sometimes snow falls from them.   ....

C ▶ Tony and Sally's favourite weather.

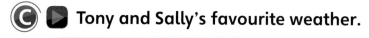

wind   sunny   windy   raining   fly   bike   ride   kite

1   Tony likes .... weather because when it is ....
he can't .... his .... to school.

2   Sally is happy when it is .... because she needs
the .... to .... her ....

D Vicky's painting class. Complete the first part of the story.

It's a _ _ _ _ _ _ day at Vicky's _ _ _ _ _ _ _ .
Vicky's in her painting _ _ _ _ _ .
She's thinking, 'What can I _ _ _ _ ?'

Now you tell the story.

Where's Vicky now?
What's she thinking about?
Has she got any ideas?

Where's Vicky now?
What's she looking at?
Has she got an idea now?

Where's Vicky now?
What's in her painting?
Who's saying, 'Well done!'

E Match sentences and story pictures. Write ①, ②, ③ or ④.

1   Wow! Look at that rainbow! It's beautiful!   picture ③

2   That's a really pretty picture, Vicky!   picture ◯

3   My friend's got a great idea but I haven't.   picture ◯

4   I can't find any good pictures in this library or on this website. Oh dear!   picture ◯

F ▶ Draw the weather.

What's it like?

Is it hot or cold?

Is it sunny or windy or cloudy?

Is it raining or snowing?

Can you see a rainbow?

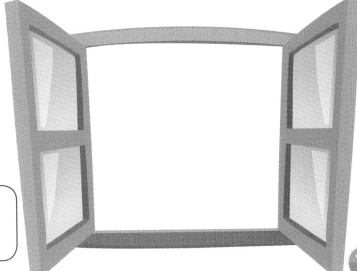

19

8 The hottest and coldest places

A ▶ Find sentence pairs about different kinds of weather.

I'm white.

I make the leaves fall from trees.

I can change things from dry to wet!

You only see me when the sun's behind you!

I come from grey clouds.

I come out when you go to bed.

Look carefully to see my seven colours.

When you see me, you can see stars, too.

You want me when you go sailing!

I only fall on really, really cold days.

I'm hot, big and round.

No, you can't see me at night!

B Listen and write and say!

Is it right to fly a kite at night?

C Complete the sentences with words from the box.

1

2

3

4

5

6

1 The .... coldest .... place in the world is Antarctica.
2 The .... town is in India. It rains there a lot!
3 Africa is the .... part of the world.
4 The .... place is Antarctica, too. The wind there is really strong!
5 In Arizona, it's always dry and sunny! It's the .... place the USA.

driest
~~coldest~~
sunniest
wettest
windiest
hottest

D Choose words to complete the weather sentences.

It is

windy
cloudy
sunny
hot
cold

today.

It was

yesterday.

It

is raining
is snowing
rained
snowed

today.

It

yesterday.

E Choose the correct words and write them on the lines.

Animals in cold parts of the world

We don't see many animals in the coldest parts of the world, but polar bears, which are

Example white, ...*live*........ in really cold places.

		lived	live	living

1 Brown bears .... when the weather is very cold.

1	sleep	sleeping	sleeps

2 .... don't wake up or eat any food.

2	It	They	We

When the weather starts getting cold, some
3 birds fly .... hotter countries, but penguins are very happy in the snow!

3	by	to	at

Snowshoe rabbits are really clever!
4 .... the weather's very cold and
5 there's snow on the ground, ...
animal's fur changes from brown to white!

4	When	Why	Which
5	those	all	this

F Which are the tallest, strongest and cleverest animals?

G Let's write funny sentences!

9 'Me and my family'

A Who are they? Listen to your teacher and draw lines.

Bill and Mary Rice

John and Anna Page

Sam and Vicky Rice

Jane (13)   Sue (11)   Ben (12)   Peter (5)

B Read about Jane. Write the family words on the lines.

My sister, Sue, and I love everyone in our family! Our parents are great! (1) ....*Dad*....'s
name is John. Our (2) ....'s called Anna. We've got a really pretty (3) ....,
too. She's called Vicky and our (4) ....'s name is Sam. He's very tall! We've got
two (5) .... They're both boys and their names are Ben and Peter.
Our (6) ....'s names are Bill and Mary. We like going to see them a lot!
They're happy because they've got four (7) .... now, Ben, Peter, Sue
and me!

C Answer questions about the people in your family.

		My answers	My friend's answers
1	Who's the oldest?	....	....
2	Who's the youngest?	....	....
3	Who's the loudest?	....	....
4	Who's the quietest?	....	....
5	Who's the cleverest?	....	....
6	Who's the busiest?	....	....
7	Who's the prettiest?	....	....
8	Who's the naughtiest?	....	....

D Write 1, 2 or 3 words to complete the sentences about the story.

On holiday at the farm

Hello! My name's Ben. I live in the town centre with my parents and my brother, Peter. Peter's younger than me. He's five and I'm twelve. Last Saturday, Dad took us all to our grandparents' farm in his car. Grandma and Grandpa live on a farm that's near the sea. We love going there.

Examples: Ben's home is in ..the town centre..

................Peter................ is Ben's brother.

1   .... is twelve years old.
2   The family went to the farm last ....
3   Ben, his brother and father travelled by ....
4   Ben's .... live near the sea.

There's always something exciting to go and see at their farm. On Sunday, my brother asked, 'Can we go and see the horses, Grandpa?' 'Yes!' Grandpa said. 'And I can show you our two new baby horses! They're only one week old. I'd like you to choose names for them!' 'Good idea!' Grandma said.

5   Ben's brother wanted to .... the horses on Sunday.
6   There were two .... on the farm.
7   Grandpa asked the boys to choose the baby horses' ....

Peter and I laughed when we saw the baby horses! They had pretty brown eyes and made funny noises when we said 'Your new names are Cloudy and Star!' On Monday, we both rode Mr Jim, grandpa's oldest horse, round the biggest field. Peter and I really loved that holiday.

8   The boys called the two baby horses ....
9   The boys rode Mr Jim round grandfather's ....
10   Ben and his brother enjoyed .... a lot!

E Can you hear the sound 'Zzzzzzzz'?

boys names who's always
answers his noises he's horses
busiest legs Thursday eyes ours

'People in our street'

A) Write ten words to put in the gaps. You choose!

Hi! I live in (1) .... Street. There are only about
(2) .... houses and flats in our street.

I don't know everyone but we're friends with the Fish family.
They live in a (3) .... white house. It's got lots of
windows and a funny (4) .... roof. Mr Fish is a
sports teacher and he likes cooking (5) .... on his
balcony! Mrs Fish gives dancing and music lessons. She can
play the (6) .... really well. She can make really great
chocolate (7) .... too!

Mr and Mrs Fish have got a son who's called (8) ....
He's got a pet (9) .... ! I really like playing
(10) .... with him in their garden after school.

B) ▶ Listen and tick (✔) the box.

Example   Which is Lily's house?

A ☐   B ☐   C ✔

1   What is Dan's father doing now?

A ☐   B ☐   C ☐

2   What are Lily and Dan playing?

A ☐   B ☐   C ☐

3   How does Dan's mother go to work?

A ☐   B ☐   C ☐

4   What is on Mr Field's balcony?

A ☐   B ☐   C ☐

5   Who is waiting at the bus stop?

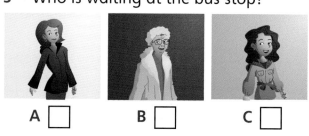

A ☐   B ☐   C ☐

C ▶ **Listen to us!**

My son, my brother, my mother and my uncle are waiting in Upunder Road for the number one bus.

D **Read and choose the best answer.**

Dan:

Example   What's the new girl's name?

Lily:

(A) It's Sally Love.
B   No, Pat's 10 now.
C   Lily can't come.

1   What's she like?

A   She likes chocolate.
B   It's her funny book.
C   She's really nice.

2   Has she got any brothers?

A   Only one, I think.
B   She never does that.
C   No, it's Charlie.

3   Tell me about her.

A   Some really loud music!
B   She's good at sport!
C   It's my book, not hers!

4   Shall I invite her to my party?

A   So do I!
B   Good idea!
C   Here you are!

5   What's her phone number?

A   Yes, she's in class 13.
B   Her phone's really great.
C   I don't know, but I can ask her.

E **Read and draw pictures of Dan, Lily and Sally.**

Dan and Lily both live in Easy Street and now Sally lives there, too. Dan's got brown eyes, but Lily's and Sally's eyes are blue and bigger than Dan's. Dan's got the biggest nose and the biggest ears, but his mouth is the smallest. Dan's hair is brown and really curly, but Lily's is blonde and straight. Sally's hair is black. It's shorter than Lily's hair but it's longer than Dan's hair!

PROJECT

11 Things we eat and drink

A Write the food and drink words in the correct box.

coconut lime burger coffee beans bread pasta chicken lemonade carrots
mango grapes apple sausages tea eggs milk cheese pear juice chocolate
ice cream fish water peas onions lemon rice watermelon

.... coconut ....

.... chicken ....
....
....
meat

.... juice ....
....
....
drinks
....

.... peas ....
VEGETABLES
....

.... pasta ....
....
....
....
....

B Say which one is different and why.

Example: Soup is different. Soup is hot.
Orange juice, lemonade and ice
cream aren't hot. They're cold.

hot/cold   meat/fruit
green/orange   eat/drink

26

C Choose the correct words and write them on the lines.

bananas   soup   a sandwich   a pineapple   coffee   sweets

Example   You find this yellow fruit on trees. Monkeys really like them!   .....*bananas*.....

1   Some people put milk and sugar in this hot drink.   ....

2   You can eat or drink this from a bowl or from a cup.   ....

3   You make this with bread and you can put meat or salad inside.   ....

4   Most children and grown ups love eating these but they are bad
      for your teeth!   ....

5   This fruit is yellow inside. You can eat it and you can make juice
      from it too.   ....

D Choose the correct words and write them on the lines.

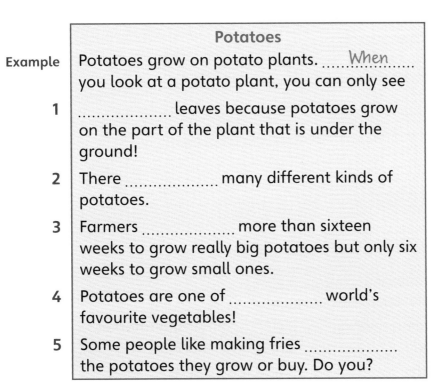

Potatoes	What	Which	When
Example Potatoes grow on potato plants. .....*When*..... you look at a potato plant, you can only see	What	Which	When
1 .... leaves because potatoes grow on the part of the plant that is under the ground!	**1** its	hers	his
2 There .... many different kinds of potatoes.	**2** is	are	was
3 Farmers .... more than sixteen weeks to grow really big potatoes but only six weeks to grow small ones.	**3** need	needs	needing
4 Potatoes are one of .... world's favourite vegetables!	**4** a	all	the
5 Some people like making fries .... the potatoes they grow or buy. Do you?	**5** by	off	with

E Talk in pairs about the food you eat.
Then, find words in words!

A **What are these? What do we put inside them? Write words.**

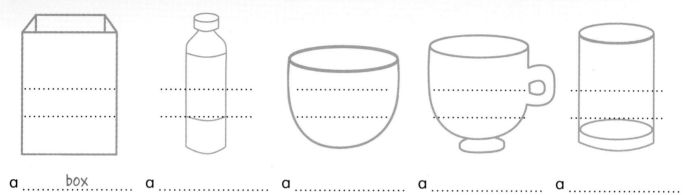

a .... box ....   a ....   a ....   a ....   a ....

B ▶ **Listen and colour and draw.**

C **Complete the sentences about the picture in B.**

> round   floor   ~~table~~   boxes   bowl   square

1   Three people are standing near a .... table .... in a supermarket.
2   Most of the bottles and .... are on the shelves.
3   The biggest box is on the .... and it is closed.
4   The .... bottle is next to the bigger bowl.
5   Four glasses are between the .... bottle and the smaller ....

D **What does Sam have to do? Listen and write words.**

Dad's birthday party!

I must

1 phone: .... Jim this afternoon
2 buy: .... bottles of lemonade
3 wash: the three purple ....
4 choose: some great ....
5 find: my ....

E **Look at the pictures. Tell the story.**

F **Read and draw the birthday party table.**

Draw a really big table. It can be round or square – you choose!

Draw some glasses, bowls, bottles, plates on top of the table.

On the outside of one of the bottles, write what is inside.

Draw a big birthday cake on a really big square plate.

Draw a birthday present on the floor.

Add lots of balloons to the picture!

Colour the picture.

A Draw lines between the words in the boxes and picture A.

door leaves trees wall roof chimney

window basement balcony stairs mat grass

B Read and choose the best answer.

Example

Sally: Hi Tony! My afternoon was great!

Tony: A Tell me about it!

B How about Saturday?

C It's better in the morning.

1 **Sally:** I went to that big old house where my uncle works.

Tony: A Yes, that's wrong.

B I know that place.

C Sorry, I can't.

2 **Sally:** They're making a movie inside the house!

Tony: A Here they are.

B How exciting!

C It's not inside.

3 **Sally:** There were lots of famous people there today!

Tony: A Really?

B I'm sorry.

C Shall I?

4 **Tony:** Is your uncle in the movie?

Sally: A No, you mustn't.

B Is it OK now?

C Yes, he is!

5 **Sally:** I helped the cameraman today!

    Tony: A No thanks.

            B Well done!

            C Come on!

6 **Sally:** I can show you part of the movie on my phone!

    Tony: A I'd like that!

            B Me too!

            C Be careful!

C **Use 1, 2 or 3 words to complete the sentences about Sally's afternoon.**

Example Sally and Tony are talking about the things that Sally did this
.... *afternoon* ....

1 Sally's uncle works in a ....

2 The people inside the house are making ....

3 Sally saw some .... there.

4 Sally worked with the .... today.

5 Sally and Tony can watch part of the movie on Sally's ....

D Find the differences between the pictures.

E Talk about the differences between the pictures.

F Play the game! Two things.

14 Our homes

A Choose words from the circle to complete what Jack says.

My .... is Jack Fine.
My .... is 78, Garden
Road. I live in a ....
in a village called Well. Our
home has six ....
We've got a kitchen, a living
room and a dining room
downstairs and two
bedrooms and a bathroom
upstairs.

people
address   rooms
tree   name
house

B Listen and write.

Ben's grandmother's new home

Colour: blue and ...... white ......
1   Number of bedrooms: ....
2   Address: ......, Bank Road
3   Name of village: ....
4   Favourite rowom: ....
5   House is near: ....

C Now write about your home.

I live in .... (an apartment / a flat / a house)
My address is ....
I live in .... (a village / a town / a city / the countryside)
Our home has .... rooms. We've got a ....
....
....
My favourite room is .... because ....
There's a .... near my home. You can .... there.

D **Answer the questions about where you live.**

1 How many windows are there? ....
2 How many phones are there? ....
3 How many floors are there? ....
4 Have you got a garden? ....
5 Does it have a lift? ....
6 Does it have stairs? ....
7 What colour is the roof? ....
8 What's in your living room? ....
....

E **Say and spell chicken and kitchen!**

t

n

k

i

c

e

h

A ⬡ is a kind of bird but it can't fly.

We eat in our ⬡ because we haven't

got a dining room in our house.

Can you say it?

Charlie the chicken is in Kim's kitchen. Charlie's eating
the chips that Kim cooked. Quick! Catch Charlie!

F Listen and draw. Who lives here?

G Draw and describe! My dream home.

PROJECT

15 'At our school'

A Choose the correct words below and write them on the lines.

Example: You can play different kinds of this on a guitar or piano. ....music....

1 This is on the classroom wall and the teacher writes on it. ....

2 These are in books and often have numbers on them at the bottom. ....

3 When you make a mistake with your pencil, you need this. ....

4 Some teachers put these at the end of correct answers in tests. ....

5 We look at these to find roads and rivers and towns. ....

Example

| music | a board | maps | a rubber | pages |

| ticks | pointed | talked | happy |

B Read the story. Write the correct word from A next to numbers 1–6.

On Tuesday morning, the ....music.... teacher, Mr Skip, came into Nick's class and said, 'Hello! I've got a message for you from Miss Sweet. She'd like you to answer the questions on (1) .... 66 and 67 for your homework. They're about the world's longest rivers.

Miss Sweet isn't in school today. She's talking on the radio about playing word and picture games in school lessons. It's very exciting!'

Mr Skip (2) .... to some orange books. 'The (3) .... in those can help you, or you can find your answers on the internet,' he said. Nick was (4) .... because he loved working on computers. That evening he found all the answers to Miss Sweet's questions on one of his favourite websites.

When Miss Sweet came back to school, she (5) .... about her exciting day, then looked at everyone's homework. 'What great answers!' she said. 'You've got lots of (6) .... and no crosses! Well done!

Now choose the best name for the story. Tick (✔) one box.

Miss Sweet buys a new radio! ☐

Nick's class get all the right answers! ☐

Mr Skip's exciting music lesson! ☐

Alex   Jack   Paul   Daisy

Grace   Tony   Fred

D **Find the sentences with mistakes.**

1   The boy in the green T-shirt is reading a book.
2   Both of the boys who are drawing on the board have got white shoes on.
3   Two of the boys are wearing yellow T-shirts.
4   The computer mouse and keyboard are on the desk.
5   The picture of the train is above one boy's head.
6   You can see a book that is closed on the floor under the table.

E **Colour your answers.**

1   How do you come to school?   by (bike)(car)(bus)(train)   (I walk)

2   Where do you do your homework?   in the (bedroom)(library)(kitchen)(living room)

3   When do you have English lessons?   on (Monday)(Tuesday)(Wednesday)
                                                      (Thursday)(Friday)(Saturday)

4   What do you like doing most in English?   (speaking)(writing)(listening)(reading)

F **Play the game! Backs to the board.**

16 'Let's do some sport!'

A Who said what? Write the words in the sentences.

Vicky

watched   laughed
shouted   watched
                    jumped
played   played
                    shouted
jumped   rained

FRED

I enjoyed Saturday!
I ....played.... tennis in the
morning and ....
a DVD in the afternoon.
In the evening, our dog
.... in some water.
Dad .... 'Don't
do that!' But it was funny.
I .... a lot!

Sunday was OK.
I .... hockey in the
morning and I ....
a football game on TV
in the afternoon. But my
mouse .... out of
its box in the evening and
Mum .... 'Help!'
It .... a lot too.

B What did Peter do last week? Listen and draw a line from the day to the correct picture.

a

b

c

d

Monday

Tuesday

Wednesday

Thursday

Friday

Saturday

Sunday

e

f

C **Find the answers to the questions. Write numbers.**

I played a different game one day.

(1) What game did you play?

(2) When?

(3) Was it fun?

◯ Yes, it was great!

◯ Baseball!

◯ On Friday.

D **Choose the correct words and write them on the lines.**

Football

Example People all round ....the.......... world play
1 football but the first people ....
played football lived in England. Did you
know that in many games, football players
2 .... about eight kilometers!

The game is called football in most countries
but in America and Canada some people
3 call .... soccer. Another name for
football is 'the beautiful game'.

One of the most famous football players
is called Lionel Messi. He could kick a
4 football really well .... he was
only five years old. You can read about him
5 .... the internet.

	the	as	this
1	whose	what	who
2	run	runs	running
3	them	it	us
4	when	because	or
5	by	at	on

E **Write the sport. You can make all the words from the letters in the sport.**
(The first letter of the first word is the first letter of the sport!)

Example b a s k e t b a l l   ball, table, skate

2 _ _ _ _ _ _ _ _   fall, boat, too, foot

3 _ _ _ _ _ _ _ _ _ _ _   ten, tail, best, table

4 _ _ _ _ _ _ _ _ _ _   bad, into, mat

5 _ _ _ _ _ _ _ _ _ _   in, nice, sing, tick, skate

6 _ _ _ _ _ _ _ _ _ _ _   hide, doing, goes, ride

How many words can you make from

sports centre

F **Choose your sport!**

37

Our hobbies

A Listen and draw lines.

Sally　　　Peter　　　Pat　　　Charlie

Mary　　　Daisy　　　John

B Write the words under the pictures. The first letter is there to help you.

1 ....hockey....　　2 s.................　　3 c.................　　4 D.................

5 a p.................　　6 s.................　　7 a r.................　　8 t.................
t.................

C Choose the correct words from B and write them on the lines.

1 This is like dancing but you do it on ice.   ....skating........
2 You can do this after you jump into a lake or a pool.   ....
3 There are funny stories and lots of pictures in these.   ....
4 You can play music on this. Part of it is black and white.   ....
5 These are films you can watch on a computer or DVD player.   ....
6 People hit a small ball that bounces in this game.   ....
7 We can listen to music or people talking on this in our car.   ....

D Choose words from B. Write the correct words next to numbers 1–5.

Vicky is my younger sister. She's really happy when the weather is sunny because she loves being outside and doing sports like ....hockey........ .

Last weekend, it snowed and Vicky went (1)........................ on the lake in the park with her friends both days.

Dan, my older brother, doesn't like hot weather and enjoys being inside. He often listens to music on the (2)........................ .

Last Saturday, he watched (3)........................ at home with his friends. The only sport Dan plays is (4)........................ in our basement with his best friend Bill.

When he's older, Dan wants to draw pictures for (5)........................ or websites. He's very good at drawing funny pictures.

E Now choose the best name for the story about Vicky and Dan. Tick (✔) one box.

My brother and sister ☐   A day at the park ☐   My favourite sport ☐

F ▶ Listen, then tell the three word story!

Lucy's beach day

Home cupboard bags
Bags car beach
Beach got out hat
Hat towel bags
Bags hello John
John boat sea

G Play the game! Draw your circle.

18 At the hospital

A Look and read. Choose the correct words and write them on the lines.

a driver

a nurse

a party

a playground

movies

a picnic

skates

a hospital

Example	You can take this with you to eat on a trip.	*a picnic*
1	This person can take you to different places in the car.	....
2	People invite their friends to this on their birthday.	....
3	You can see these at a cinema, on a DVD or computer.	....
4	Many doctors work at this place.	....
5	Children can run and climb outside here.	....
6	This person takes your temperature when you aren't well.	....

B Answer the questions.

1 What was the last birthday party you went to? What did you do?
2 What's your favourite movie? Which famous people are in the movie?
3 What food and drink do you take when you have a picnic?
4 What's the name of the nearest hospital? Is it a big hospital?
5 Is someone in your family a dentist, a nurse or a doctor?

C Choose the best words and complete the sentences.

1 Sometimes, when you are not .... and
your body is ...., you have a temperature.

hot   well
cold

2 When your mum has a .... headache,
it's a good idea to be very .... at home.

bad   quiet
tired

3 Be .... when you're hungry! Tony ate five
chocolate ice creams on Sunday and then he had a
.... stomach-ache!

dirty   terrible
careful

D Look and read. Write yes or no.

Example	The room where the people are waiting is busy. ...yes...
1	The doctor who is looking at the baby has got curly hair. ....
2	The plant that the boy is holding is very big. ....
3	The nurse who is wearing glasses is talking to a doctor. ....
4	The seat which is between the boy and the baby has a bag on it. ....
5	You can see the faces of everyone who is in this room. ....

Now write who, where or that in these sentences.

6 The man .... is talking on the phone is sitting down.

7 The comic .... the girl has got in her hands is open.

8 The place .... you can buy coffee is closed.

E Listen and colour and draw.

F Play the game! Find the silent letters.

temperature

stomach   **talk**

friends

head

19 What's the matter?

A **Write e, i, o or u on the lines to complete the words and sentences.**

1 __'v__ g__t a st__mach-ach__ b__ca__s__ __ at__ h__ndr__ds of ch__ps at sch__ __l t__day.

2 W__ walk__d a l__t y__st__rday and n__w b__th my f__ __t h__rt.

3 Wh__n my c__ __s__n and __ w__nt skat__ng last w__ __k, I h__rt my hand and h__ h__rt h__s ....

B **Read the sentences. Write the number and letter of the pictures in C.**

1 This woman hurt her arm this morning. ....4C.........
2 This boy was outside in the wind yesterday. Now he's got earache. ....
3 Oh dear! That woman hurt her hand. Now she can't play basketball. ....
4 That man doesn't look well. He's got a temperature. ....
5 This boy needs to see a dentist. He's got very bad toothache. ....
6 This man carried a lot of big boxes from the car. Now his back hurts. ....
7 Give that girl a glass of water, please! She's got a cough. ....
8 That man always eats too quickly. Now he's got a stomach-ache. ....

C ▶ **Listen and tick (✔) the box.**

1 What's the matter with Ben?

A ☐   B ☐   C ☐

2 What was the matter with Kim today?

A ☐   B ☐   C ☐

3 What's the matter with Dad?

A ☐   B ☐   C ☐

4 Why did Mum go to hospital?

A ☐   B ☐   C ☐

D Read and choose the best answer.

Example

Sue: Hello, Tom. How are you?

Tom: (A) Fine, thanks!

     B Well done!

     C That's good!

Questions

1 Sue: Why weren't you at school yesterday?

    Tom: A That is today's lesson.

          B It's in our street.

          C I went to hospital.

2 Sue: What was the matter?

    Tom: A It's not mine.

          B I hurt my foot.

          C You asked me.

3 Tom: The nurse was really nice.

    Sue: A Was she?

          B Here you are!

          C Where is it?

4 Sue: So, are you all right?

    Tom: A Yes! Don't worry!

          B I can walk there!

          C OK, I can tell you!

5 Sue: What are you doing now?

    Tom: A I'd like to do that.

          B Waiting for my dad.

          C Next to the phone.

E Find five differences between Tom and Paul.

F Write answers to the questions about Paul.

1 Why didn't Paul come to school today?   _He had to go to hospital._

2 What's the matter with him?   ....

3 How did he do that?   ....

4 Where is he now?   ....

G Saying 'ch'.

Charlie chose a cheese sandwich for lunch.
Kim ate a lot of carrot cake then she had a stomach-ache!

43

20 'Where?'

A Write the words under the pictures.

a shop   a lift   a farm   a supermarket   the sea   a river   a market   stairs
a hospital   a bank   a beach   a mountain   ~~a playground~~   a lake   a classroom

1
a *a playground*   b ....   c ....   d ....

2
a ....   b ....   c ....   d ....

3
a ....   b ....   c ....   d ....

4
a ....   b ....   c ....   d ....

5
a ....   b ....   c ....   d ....

B Which picture is different and why?

C Read the story. Choose a word from the box. Write the correct word next to numbers 1–6.

Example

sunny   sandwiches   juice   give   afraid

walk   loud   lake   doctor

Fred and Grace live in the town centre but on ....sunny........ days, they sometimes go for bike rides in the countryside. Last Saturday, they rode to a small (1) .... and jumped about on the rocks next to the water there. Fred saw three ducks on a small island. 'Come here, ducks!' he shouted. But the ducks didn't come because they were (2) .... of the noise. 'Don't worry about the ducks now, Fred!' Grace said. 'Let's sit down. I've got some apple (3) .... in my bag to drink. Do you want some?', she asked. 'Yes! I'm really thirsty,' Fred answered. 'Let's eat all our cheese (4) .... now, too.

Grace took the food out of her bag. 'Look!' she said. Those ducks aren't frightened now. They can see our picnic! Shall we (5) .... them some of our bread?'

'Good idea!' said Fred. 'Come on, you clever ducks! There's lots for you to eat here!

'I love animals!' Grace laughed. 'I want to be a (6) .... one day – I'd like to help animals get better, not people!'

Choose the best name for the story. Tick (✔) one box.

Grace's new bike   ☐

Mum has a picnic   ☐

Fred's duck friends   ☐

D Make your pictures the same!

E Find the *k*'s! Look at the words in A and C.
Put a line under all the *k*'s you find.

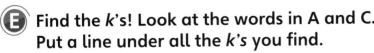

21 Here and there in town

A **Where can you go to do these things in town?**

go for a swim   **catch buses**   **buy fruit**

choose books   **see a doctor**

B Look and read. Choose the correct words and write them on the lines.

a supermarket

coffee

soup

a café

a zoo

milk

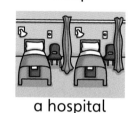
a hospital

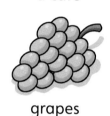
grapes

Example

People go here to see different animals like bears and tigers. ....a zoo.......

1   There are lots of beds in this place. Doctors work here. ....

2   You can make this from vegetables then put it in a bowl. ....

3   People sit and have a drink and talk to their friends here. ....

4   This fruit can be red or green. You can eat it or drink its juice. ....

5   You can buy lots of different food in this large store. ....

6   Mothers often give this white drink to babies. ....

C Read Jane's postcard and write the correct words.

Hi Grandpa!

It's great here!

We didn't go to the beach this morning. We drove to the town to go for a walk there. We had lunch there too. We found a café near the market with lots of chairs outside. Mum had pea soup and Dad and I had salad. Then we went to the market to buy some fruit. Mum bought a new handbag there too. It's the end of the afternoon now and we're in the park. Mum's sleeping under a big tree! Oh! Dad wants to play badminton now! I've got to go! See you!

Love Jane XX

bought

walked ~~town~~

tennis lunch

badminton sleeping

shopping father

1 Jane and her family went to the ....town........ this morning.
2 They had .... in a café that was near the market.
3 Jane's .... had some salad in the café.
4 They .... some fruit and a handbag in the market.
5 Jane's mother is .... in the park now.
6 Jane's father wants to have a game of .... in the park.

D ▶ **Listen and tick (✔) the box.**

Example Where does May's brother work?

A ☐   B ☐   C ✔

1 Which is Kim's dad?

A ☐   B ☐   C ☐

2 Where did Dan have lunch?

A ☐   B ☐   C ☐

3 What is Lily doing?

A ☐   B ☐   C ☐

4 What is Aunt Lucy doing?

A ☐   B ☐   C ☐

5 Where is Charlie's bag?

A ☐   B ☐   C ☐

E **Listen and say!**

Super soup, juice and beautiful fruit too for you at the new Super Food Supermarket!

F **Play the game! Connecting words.**

A Write sentences about a village and a city.

A village	A city
Not many people live here	

Thousands of people live here. Homes are often newer. Most gardens are bigger. People often walk more quickly. Streets are often longer here. It's quieter here. Sometimes farms are near here. Roads are often shorter. There are big shopping centres. People often walk more slowly. Homes are often older. It's noisier here. Not many people have gardens. Sometimes there's a shop here. Schools have lots of classrooms.

B What did Daisy do last week?
Listen and draw a line from the day to the correct picture.

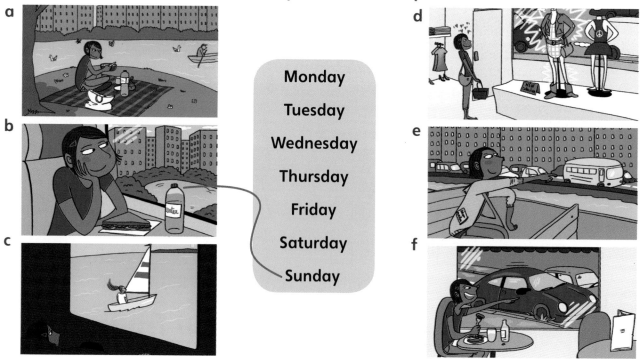

a
b
c

Monday
Tuesday
Wednesday
Thursday
Friday
Saturday
Sunday

d
e
f

C Questions! What's really quiet? What moves quickly?

D Listen and look. Write **yes** or **no**.

Examples: One of the boys is pointing at something. ...yes....
You can only see one person on the motorbike. .....no.....

1 The clown is standing between two children. ....
2 The bigger car is in front of the smaller car. ....
3 A woman is waiting at the bus stop in this street. ....
4 A girl is climbing up the tree to help the black cat. ....
5 There are more than two keyboards in the shop window. ....
6 The person with the guitar is wearing red trousers. ....

E I think I know the answer!
Is the right answer green or purple?

PROJECT

I think this city is a really exciting place!

So do I.

Because he's funny.

Do you want to go there?

I know there is a bookshop near here.

It's about to go to the moon.

No, it isn't in this road.

I think we need to find a café. I'm hungry!

And I'm really thirsty!

Outside the shopping centre.

I know that's the right bus. Quick! Come on!

OK!

A Draw circles round the things that you can see in the picture.

a farm	fields	flowers	rocks
grass	an island	a jungle	stars
clouds	the moon	a waterfall	plants

B Read the sentences. What things in the picture are they about?

1 People like walking or climbing up these when they are on holiday. ....
2 You can swim and sail here, but it is not a river or the sea. ....
3 There are always lots of trees, animals and birds here. ....
4 You find these on trees and plants. They are green, red, yellow or brown. ....
5 People live in houses here. It's smaller than a town. ....
6 Go outside in the day, look up and see this! It's big, hot, yellow and round. ....

C  Listen and colour and draw.

D Read and cross out the wrong words.

Jungles

Jungles are (1) *cold / hot*, and (2) *dry / wet* places. They are very (3) *green / pink / black* because it (4) *never / often / carefully* rains there. A lot of flowers, plants and (5) *animals / puppies / pets* live in jungles. There are big (6) *rivers / seas / streets* in lots of jungles. Be careful, because sometimes you can find (7) *crocodiles / whales / dolphins* in some of them!

Many people who live in a jungle have their homes next to a river or a waterfall because they need (8) *soup / tea / water*. People often go up or down the river by (9) *boat / truck / motorbike*. Rivers are like roads in a jungle.

E Write g or j to complete the words, then say the sentences!

There are some _g_reat __reen __rapes in __race's __randma's __arden.

_J_ill's __iraffe en__oys ve__etables and __ungle __uice!

F Do the *World Around Us* quiz!

24 Travelling, texting, phoning

A **Look at picture a. What do you think? Write yes or no?**

1 The man is in the countryside. ....
2 It's a very cloudy day. ....
3 Two things are flying in this picture. ....
4 The man came to this place by car. ....
5 The weather is really cold there. ....

a

B **Picture a or b? Read the sentences and write a or b.**

1 There are no leaves on the trees. .....b.....
2 There's only one cloud. ....
3 The helicopter is on the ground. ....
4 The man's hair is straight. ....
5 You can see a red car. ....
6 The duck is bigger. ....
7 The man is pointing at the helicopter. ....
8 The mat is square. ....
9 The man is wearing a blue shirt. ....

b

C **Complete the sentences.**

1 In picture **a**, there's one cloud, but in picture **b**, there are ....two............ clouds.
2 In picture **b**, the man's got blond hair but in **a**, he's got .... hair.
3 In **b**, the picnic mat is square, but in **a**, it's ....
4 In picture **a**, the helicopter's flying, but in **b**, it's on the ....
5 In picture **b**, the car's ...., but in picture **a**, it's ....
6 In **a**, the man's shirt is .... but in **b** it's ....
7 In picture **a**, the trees have got ...., but in **b**, they ....

D Write the letters of the alphabet to complete the words.

a																									z
			5						10															25	

1   13 5 19 19 1 7 5
     m e s s̲ a g e̲

2   9 14 20 5 18 14 5 20
     i n t _ r n̲ _ _

3   5 13 1 9 12
     _ _ _ _ l̲

4   20 5 24 20
     _ _ x̲ _

5   22 9 4 5 15
     v̲ _ _ _ o̲

6   23 5 2 19 9 20 5
     w̲ _ b̲ _ _ _ _

7   16 8 15 20 15 19
     p̲ h̲ _ _ _ _

E Write the words from D in Nick's sentences.

Nick is phoning his work friend May to tell her about his trip.

I'm calling you because I (4) ......texted...... you this morning but I don't think you got my (1) ....

> No, I didn't.

And I can't (3) .... you because there's no (2) .... here.

> Don't worry!

I've got lots of (7) .... on my phone because I'm taking pictures of everything.

> Great!

I made a really exciting (5) .... of a beautiful waterfall yesterday.

> Wow!

I'd like to add the (7) .... and the (5) .... to our (6) ....

> Good idea!

F Let's find things that we all like and do!

53

25 Which one is different?

Ⓐ Write words for the pictures, draw another picture and complete the sentence.

1 A ......plane......,
a .... and
a .... can fly.

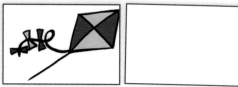

2 The three men have got
....

3 The ....,
the .... and the
.... are orange.

4 You can find an ....,
a .... and a
.... in a living room.

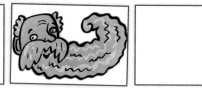

Ⓑ Say which picture is different and why.

1

2

3

4

5

54

C Read the story. Choose a word from the box. Write the correct word next to numbers 1–6.

Daisy ..... loved ..... animals. Lots of her friends had pets and Daisy wanted one too. One day she read a story in a (1) .... about a boy who had a horse. Daisy had an idea. 'Mum,' she said, 'I want to learn to (2) .... a horse. Can we have a horse?'

'Sorry, Daisy,' her mother answered. 'We can't have a horse. We haven't got a field.' 'What about a kitten, then?' Daisy asked. 'My friend, Sally, has got a cat.' 'No Daisy,' her mother said. 'We (3) .... in a flat. Cats like being in gardens.'

Daisy went and sat on the balcony. She wasn't happy. But then she saw a really sweet (4) .... lizard on the ground between the two pretty green (5) .... there. 'Hello!' she said. 'Do you want to be my new pet?' The lizard looked at Daisy and moved its (6) .... up and down. 'Wow! It's saying yes!' laughed Daisy. 'It's different from all my friends' pets, but that's OK!'

Example

loved   head   plants

grey   cloudy   ride

downstairs   comic   live

Now choose the best name for the story. Tick (✔) one box.

Sally moves to a different flat [ ]   Daisy finds a pet [ ]   Mum writes a story [ ]

D Choose words for the horse and the cat.

Daisy's lizard was *really sweet* and the plants were *pretty and green*.

Now choose words for the boy's horse and Sally's cat:

Daisy read a story about a boy who had a	nice	big	black	horse.
		small	brown	
	beautiful	strong	grey	
Daisy's friend Sally has got a		clever	orange	cat.
	ugly	naughty	white	

E Play the game! Make groups of words.

26 'Guess who lives here?'

A **Look and read. Write yes or no.**

1 The biggest bat in the picture is flying below the fan. ...yes...
2 There's a green bat at the bottom of the stairs and it's sleeping ....
3 Two bats are outside the house. ....
4 You can see a bat in front of the window. ....
5 The smallest bat in the picture is on top of the phone. ....
6 In this picture, we can only see one spider. ....
7 The bat which is above the hall table is brown. ....
8 Most of the bats are inside the house. ....

Quick Cloud Dream Teeth Sandwich

B **Listen and draw lines between the names and the bats.**

C Read and then write the names of the people who live in each flat.

Mr and Mrs White live at the bottom of the stairs, below Mary Pink. The White family like cooking a lot. They often invite friends to their flat and they have dinner parties.

Anna and Bill Brown love reading quietly in their living room. They don't like living above Miss Green because she plays very loud music when she comes home after work.

Miss Green lives opposite her friend Mary Pink. They are both learning to play the guitar and they make a lot of noise.

John Grey's flat is under Miss Green's. He doesn't have to drive to work because he works on his website at home but he rides round the park on his bike every morning first.

The newest person in this house is Lucy Blue. She moved into the flat at the top of the stairs, two floors above Mr and Mrs White's apartment.

D Play the game! Alphabet find and draw.

E From top to bottom!

PROJECT

27 Seeing differences

A Make sentences about the things in the pictures.

You find		outside windows in some houses or flats.
	this	on your head in cold weather.
You see		inside bookshops and libraries.
		on your feet when you go for a walk.
You put		at the cinema or at home on TV.
	these	in the sea or in a lake.
		on the sand on beaches.
You wear		on plants and trees.

B Find the words in the box and write them on the lines.

Example   This is green and cows and horses eat it. ....*grass*........

1   You see this on the ground at the beach. ....

2   People wear these on their feet, but they don't walk in them! ....

3   Bands sometimes write these. They're music with words. ....

4   Some people have these when they are asleep. ....

5   You can call people on this and talk to them.   a ....

6   Some men have this under their nose and above their mouths.   a ....

7   You run a lot and kick a ball in this game.   ....

8   This is hair that some men have at the bottom of their face, below their mouth.   a ....

d	r	e	a	m	s	m
n	b	e	a	r	d	o
s	k	a	t	e	s	u
g	l	a	s	s	e	s
s	o	c	c	e	r	t
b	v	s	a	n	d	a
i	s	o	n	g	s	c
k	p	h	o	n	e	h
e	g	r	a	s	s	e

C Say which picture is different and why.

D Listen and write your answers, then complete the story.

Last night, I watched a video on my computer of (1) .... singing
(7) .... Then, because I was really hungry, I ate (5) .... plates of
(4) .... (6) .... That afternoon, I didn't go to (2) ....
to play (3) .... because I couldn't move my (9) .... and my
stomach hurt too! That night, I had a funny dream about (8) .... naughty
(10) .... In my dream, they skipped and hopped outside my room on the
balcony. They danced to (7) .... too!

E Play the game! Plural quiz.

28 Our busy holidays

A ▶ Listen and draw lines and then complete the sentences.

(Monday) (Tuesday) (Wednesday) (Thursday) (Friday) (Saturday) (Sunday)

1 On .... , Alex climbs mountains and the weather is sometimes
   ....

2 Alex always paints walls with his .... John on ....

3 Alex sometimes videos his .... Lucy when she plays basketball on
   ....

4 Alex always has helicopter lessons with his .... Mary on
   ....

5 Fridays are exciting too because Alex and his uncle ....

B Answer the questions.

1 Where do you go in
   the school holidays?

   A ☐   B ☐   C ☐

2 What do you wear?

   A ☐   B ☐   C ☐

3 Who do you see?   my family   my friends   my teacher

   A ☐   B ☐   C ☐

C **Choose a word from the box. Write the correct word next to numbers 1–5.**

Hello! I'm Alex's daughter, ... and I'm ten. My brother .... is a year younger than I am.

In the school holidays, our parents always take us to exciting places like to the lake or the beach! We often go ..... _sailing_ ..... on our boat there. We love (1) .... and playing in the water. We like fishing in the (2) .... too, but we never catch any big fish!

Our dog, Jack, always comes with us. Sometimes, we (3) .... Jack's ball and he tries to find it. He loves doing that! Last year we took Jack on a balloon and helicopter ride! When he was a puppy, Jack was really (4) .... of flying, but now he isn't!

We like watching movies on our DVD player and playing (5) .... on the internet but we don't do those things in the school holidays because we think it's more exciting to be outside.

What do you like doing in your school holidays?

Example

sailing   song   hide   swimming

frightened   tennis   games   river   pretty

D **Write the correct words on the lines then ask four questions.**

.... _make_ .... a cake   .... _eat_ .... a cake
watch a ....   go .... for clothes
listen to your favourite ....
phone your best ....   go for a long ....
draw a .... by plane

make   eat   shopping   video   travel
friend   walk   band   picture

E **Play the game! Who, what, when, where?**

29 About us

A **Look at the pictures. Complete the sentences.**

 That man sings very ....

 That man is driving very ....

B **What do you think? Write yes or no.**

1   People in my country drive slowly.   ....
2   Everyone in my family talks quietly.   ....
3   I always carry things carefully.   ....
4   My parents dance very badly.   ....
5   Our teacher sings very well.   ....
6   Our class is learning English very quickly. ....
7   Music is better when people play it loudly. ....

yes answers [   ]   no answers [   ]

C **Find words that start with these letters in the picnic picture.**

c d p

D ▶ **Listen and draw lines.**

Mary   John   Daisy   Sally

Tony   Bill   Vicky

E Read the story. Choose words.

John's trip to the castle

I walked to the castle <u>quickly</u> /(slowly). My feet hurt because I [1] <u>had / didn't have</u> any shoes on!

When I got to the castle, I bought a big lemon ice cream because I [2] <u>was / wasn't</u> hot and hungry. But then, because I [3] <u>held / didn't hold</u> it carefully, I dropped it! I was angry after that. I [4] <u>sat / didn't sit</u> down on a seat inside the castle because I was really tired after my long walk. I fell asleep and had a dream.

In my dream, a monster came into the castle, looked at me and then shouted something very [5] <u>loudly / quietly</u>. I was [6] <u>sad / surprised</u> but I wasn't [7] <u>frightened / thirsty</u> because the monster smiled at me! He took me into the castle kitchen and gave me lots of lemon ice cream in a [8] <u>big / bigger</u> pink bowl. I [9] <u>dropped / didn't drop</u> my ice cream on the floor again because I [10] <u>ate / didn't eat</u> it very carefully. It was great!

F Ask and answer questions.

		Me	....
1	Can you swim?	....	....
2	Are you good at running?	....	....
3	Can you cook?	....	....
4	Are you good at shouting?	....	....
5	Do you eat slowly?	....	....

G Play the game! Draw the sentences.

30 About me

A ▶ Listen and tick (✔) the questions that Miss White asks. Then listen again and write Bill's answers.

B Answer questions 1–4. Ask your friend questions 5–12.

		Bill	you
	Let's talk about you.		
1	How old are you?	....	....
2	How many brothers and sisters have you got?	....	....
3	What's your favourite colour?	....	....
4	How often do you see your friends?	....	....
	Let's talk about your school.		<u>your friend</u>
5	Who do you sit next to in class?	....	....
6	How many lessons do you have?	....	....
7	How do you come to school?	....	....
8	Where do you do your homework?	....	....
9	Which is your favourite school day?	....	....
	Let's talk about the things you like.		<u>your friend</u>
10	What's your favourite film?	....	....
a	*When did you see the film?*	....	....
b	*Where did you see it?*	....	....
c	*Who did you see the film with?*	....	....
d	*Why do you like the film? Is it funny, exciting?*	....	....
11	Do you like music?	....	....
a	*Can you play the piano or the guitar?*	....	....
b	*Are you good at singing?*	....	....
12	Can you swim?	....	....

C **What is this about? Write the same word in all the boxes!**

Lessons
—— **make you cleverer** ——

In every country in the world, people make and listen to [   ].

In many schools, children have [   ] lessons. In their classes, they can learn to sing songs and to play [   ] on the piano or guitar.

But did you know that learning [   ] can help your reading, spelling and maths too?

In the USA, grown-ups tested 90 school children.

Children who had more [   ] and Art lessons got better marks in Maths. Their reading was better too!

D **Look, read and do!**

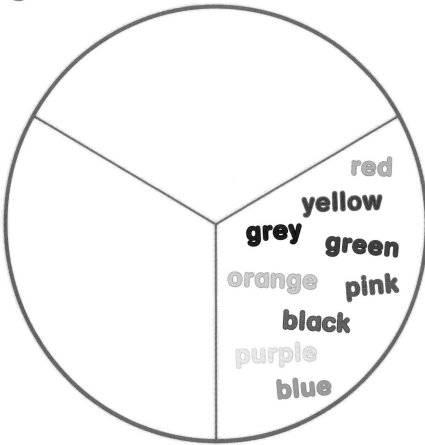

1
How many words for colours are there? Say the colour – not the word you read!

2
Write the sports that your class likes playing and watching in the top part.

3
In the bottom part, write two of your favourite foods and put a star * next to them. Then, write which fruit juice you like drinking. Draw a smiley ☺ after that! And last, write something you <u>don't</u> like eating. Then, draw a sad face ☹ after that!

E **Play the game! On my right and on my left.**

31 'Why is Sally crying?'

A **Look and read.
Write yes or no.**

Ann

Tony

Sue

Ben

Mary

Fred

Examples

We can see a monkey in a cage.	...yes...
The zebra is eating the leaves from the biggest tree.	no
1 Everyone in this picture is happy.	....
2 One of the girls is frightened of the spider.	....
3 The robot is the one who is bouncing a ball.	....
4 Three people in the picture are laughing.	....
5 The boy who is on the ground has got a headache.	....
6 The snail's climbing up the wall.	....

B ▶ **Listen and colour and write.**

C **Listen and draw lines.**

D Look at the pictures and complete and tell the story.

1

....

2

....

3

....

4

...*a*...

John's got a baby sister called Sally. Sally's only four years old. (1) Sally is really
......*sad*...... because she wants to play with her favourite teddy bear. But her teddy
bear's really .... (2) Sally's teddy bear is in some .... now because
Sally's mum is .... it. (3) Sally's mother is putting the teddy bear outside in the
.... She's putting two wet .... outside too.
(4) Now, Sally is very .... because her teddy bear is dry and very ....

> **Example**
> sad   water   garden   washing   dirty   socks   happy   clean   crying

Write the letters under the correct picture.

Mum says ...
a   Here's your bear. It's clean now!
b   Your bear needs a bath.
c   Look! Your bear's outside in the garden!
d   Your bear was dirty! This water's black!

E Read about Mr and Mrs Cook's naughty daughter Lily and draw lines.

What did Lily do this morning?   I know!
Who did she go to the beach with?   Because she got very cold.
When did she come home?   She's having a hot shower.
Where is she now?   Her two new friends from school.
Why is she having a hot shower?   She went to the beach.
How did she get cold?   She came home for lunch.
She's a naughty daughter sometimes!   She jumped off a rock into the cold
                                   water with all her clothes on.

F Play the game! Match the cards.

Mary goes shopping

A What's in the kitchen? Make sentences.

There's …
There are …

only   a lot of   not much   some   any

B Put a tick (✔) or a (✗) next to the things Mary needs to buy.

potatoes ✔   coffee   tea   rice   pasta   oranges
apples   carrots   cheese   onions   tomatoes

C Complete the sentences about the story.

Picture 1 Mary's at the ....*market*........ . She's buying some fruit and ....
for her mum. A man's giving Mary a bag of .... John Park is next to Mary.
He's got his bike with him.

Picture 2 Mary's walking home from the market. But all the .... and
.... aren't in her bag! Some of them are on the ground. .... 's
going home too. He's behind Mary.

Now, write words from the box on the lines for picture 3.

angry   market   surprised   everything   home   nothing

Mary's at .... now. Her mum's .... with her because there's .... in the bag. Mary's very .... 'I don't understand, Mum!
I put .... into the bag at the .... ' she says.

Answer the questions about picture 4.

1   Where are Mary and her mum now?   ....
2   Who's outside their house?   ....
3   What's inside the box?   ....
4   Are Mary and her mum happy now?   ....

D   Who says this? Write Mary, Mary's mum or John Park.

1   .... Mary .... : Can I have two kilos of potatoes, please?
2   .... : Where are the fruit and vegetables? This bag is empty!
3   .... : You dropped these fruit and vegetables in the street, I think.
4   .... : Thank you! Now I don't have to go shopping again!

E   Choose the correct words and write them on the lines.

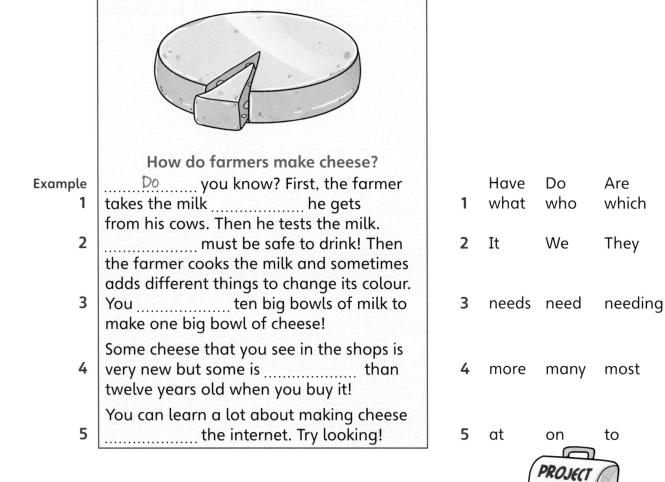

How do farmers make cheese?

Example   .... Do .... you know? First, the farmer
1   takes the milk .... he gets
    from his cows. Then he tests the milk.
2   .... must be safe to drink! Then
    the farmer cooks the milk and sometimes
    adds different things to change its colour.
3   You .... ten big bowls of milk to
    make one big bowl of cheese!
    Some cheese that you see in the shops is
4   very new but some is .... than
    twelve years old when you buy it!
    You can learn a lot about making cheese
5   .... the internet. Try looking!

	Have	Do	Are
1	what	who	which
2	It	We	They
3	needs	need	needing
4	more	many	most
5	at	on	to

PROJECT

33 'Last weekend, last week'

A Write the places under the pictures.

a pool   ~~a hospital~~   a cinema   a park   a sports centre   shops   a house

1 ....*a hospital*.... 2 .... 3 .... 4 ....

5 .... 6 .... 7 ....

....

B Paul's week. Listen and write one word on each line.

1 On Tuesday, Paul was at the ....*pool*........ with his school ....
2 On Friday afternoon, Paul went .... in the ....
3 On Saturday, Paul saw a .... with his .... John.
4 On Wednesday, Paul went shopping for .... with his ....
5 Paul went to see his friend's baby .... at the .... too.

C Let's talk about last weekend.

Where were you on Saturday?
Who were you with on Saturday afternoon?
Where did you go on Sunday?
What was the weather like on Sunday?
Tell me more about last weekend.

boring   busy   different
exciting   great   quiet   terrible

Last weekend was .... !

D Read and choose the best answer.

Example

Nick: Did you enjoy your trip last week, Paul?

Paul: (A) It was great!
    B   Saturday and Sunday!
    C   What a nice smile!

Questions

1   Nick: Which was the best day?
    Paul: A   Hers is the best one.
            B   I can go this evening.
            C   They were all good.

2   Nick: How did you travel?
    Paul: A   There were nine people.
            B   We went by plane.
            C   It was very quick.

3   Nick: Were you afraid?
    Paul: A   No, I wasn't.
            B   It's not mine.
            C   There isn't any.

4   Nick: Was the weather good?
    Paul: A   Yes, really nice every day.
            B   Yes, I like it a lot.
            C   That's nice. Well done!

5   Nick: Did you take any photos?
    Paul: A   I'm OK, thanks.
            B   No, she doesn't.
            C   Yes, forty-five!

6   Nick: You must show me them!
    Paul: A   Good night!
            B   All right!
            C   I'm sorry.

E Look and find words with *w*!

r	a	i	n	b	o	w	l	s	w
s	w	w	h	a	l	e	i	a	i
w	o	e	y	c	l	o	w	n	n
e	b	e	e	w	o	r	l	d	d
a	s	k	l	b	h	t	o	w	n
t	i	e	l	r	c	s	w	i	m
e	t	n	o	o	c	o	w	c	w
r	e	d	w	w	a	t	c	h	o
w	a	l	k	n	w	s	n	o	w

....

....

34 'What did you do then?'

A Read and circle Fred and Daisy's verbs. Then, add –ed or –d.

jump

call

wait

show

shout

plant

move

play

help

change

B Look at the pictures, then complete the sentences.

1   I p_layed_ tennis last Monday.
2   My brother p..................... all his friends last night to talk about football.
3   My younger sister c..................... six pictures with her new pencils today.
4   My big sister d..................... to some great music at a party yesterday.
5   My father w..................... a lot at the bank on Tuesday and Wednesday.
6   My cousin Jack s..................... down the river on Saturday.
7   My cousin Alex l..................... a lot at the clowns in the circus yesterday.
8   My uncle Tom c..................... lunch for all the family last Sunday.
9   My older brother d..................... six eggs on the floor last night.
10 My parents c..................... three mountains on their last holiday.

C ▶ **What did Jim do last week?**
Listen and draw a line from the day to the correct picture.

Monday

....

Wednesday

....

Friday

Saturday

Sunday

D **Complete Jim's message.**

day   dressed   shoes   nose   clown

Here we are on Thursday. It was a great ....day.... !
My uncle gave me and my friend, Ben a present.
We opened it and found some .... clothes
inside. We .... up in the clothes. My uncle
put on a big red .... He was really funny!
I put on some really big green .... I walk
very well! We all laughed and laughed!

E **Find five differences between the pictures.**

1

2

F **Play the game! Who did this?**

35 What a morning!

(A) **Choose the correct words and write them on the lines.**

a cup

breakfast

a bus stop

homework

places

a shower

a classroom

stairs

Example

Children sit at desks and learn in this place.   *a classroom*

Questions

1   You can walk up or down these inside your home.   ....

2   Wait here and then a driver takes you to town.   ....

3   People eat this in the morning. It isn't lunch!   ....

4   You stand in this and wash your body.   ....

5   You put hot coffee in this, then you pick it up and drink from it.   ....

6   You can buy a map or look on the internet to find these.   ....

(B) **Look at the pictures and tell the story of Ben's terrible school morning.**

C **Read about things we do every day.**
Complete the sentences about Ben's morning.

Every day	Ben's terrible morning
We wake up.	Ben .... *woke* .... up late.
1 We get up and we have a shower.	Ben .... up but he .... a shower.
2 We put on our school clothes and have breakfast.	Ben .... on his school clothes, but he .... breakfast.
3 We put all our school things in our school bags.	Ben .... all his school things in his school bag.
4 We put on our coats and say goodbye to our parents.	Ben .... on his coat and he .... to his parents.
5 We go out of the house and we catch the bus.	Ben .... out of the house but he .... the bus.
6 We get on the bus.	Ben .... on the bus.
7 We go into the classroom and our teacher is happy with us.	Ben .... into the classroom but his teacher .... happy.

D ▶ **Complete Nick's story. Write one word on each line.**

I got up and I (1) .... *had* .... a shower. I (2) .... on my clothes and went downstairs to the kitchen. I had breakfast with my family. Then I (3) .... my coat from the hall cupboard. I (4) .... goodbye to my parents and then I (5) .... out of the house. I walked to the bus stop and I (6) .... the bus to school. I (7) .... down on the bus and laughed and talked with my friends. When I (8) .... into the classroom, the teacher (9) .... very happy because I had all my books and homework. Ben came into the classroom. He (10) .... wet. The teacher wasn't happy with Ben because he didn't have any books or homework!

E **Play the game! The past verb game.**

36 Could you do it?

A Look at the things Sam wanted to do last Saturday. Complete the sentences.

Saturday
- play football with Paul
- do homework
- clean bike
- buy present far Sally
- email Jack and Daisy
- go to Sally's party

1 Sam ...*couldn't play football*... with Paul.
2 He .... a present for his friend.
3 He .... Jack and Daisy.
4 His bike was dirty but he .... it.
5 He was angry because he .... to Sally's party.
6 He .... any homework, but he wasn't angry about that!

B Listen and tick (✔) the box.

1 Where did Sam go this afternoon?

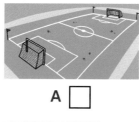  

A ☐   B ☐   C ☐

2 What did Sam do this morning?

A ☐   B ☐   C ☐

3 Where is Sam's computer?

A ☐   B ☐   C ☐

4 What homework does Sam have to do today?

A ☐   B ☐   C ☐

5 What number is Sally's house?

A ☐   B ☐   C ☐

C Draw lines from the words to the pictures.

glasses

fish

wind

lost

dropped

bag

dinner

panda

D Choose words from C to complete the sentences.

Example

I couldn't do my homework because my dog hid my
..........glasses.......... and I couldn't see.

I couldn't do my homework because ...

1 my pet .... ate
my books for ....

2 my books fell out of my
school ....

3 the .... was very strong
when I walked home from school.

4 I .... my books
in the river.

5 I .... my pen.

E Play the game! Put out the washing!

37

'Mr Must changes his job'

A **Put the words into the circles.**

I like ...

I have to ...

have/having a shower

eat/eating breakfast

go/going to school

clean/cleaning my teeth

stay/staying in bed

sleep/sleeping

get/getting undressed

watch/watching TV

do/doing homework

play/playing computer games

dry/drying plates

B **Read the story and write words to complete the sentences.**

Mr Must's exciting letter

John Must was a bus driver. He didn't like getting up in the morning but he couldn't stay in bed! Mrs Must woke him up. She said 'Get up, John!' After breakfast every morning he had to put on his bus driver's uniform and ride his bike to work in the town centre.

When he got to the bus station, he had to wash the bus. Then he had to start the bus and drive it all day. He had to say 'Good morning!' and smile at the people who got on his bus at every bus stop.

But Mr Must didn't want to be a bus driver. He wanted to work in the countryside.

Example Mr Must .... *woke* .... John up in the morning.

1 Mr Must went to work on his .... every day.

2 John washed and started the bus, then he had to .... it round the town all day.

3 Mr Must said .... to all the people on the bus.

4 Mr Must didn't like being a ....

One evening, when he got home, Mrs Must said, 'A letter came for you today. Here you are!' Mr Must opened his letter and smiled. 'Wow!' he said. 'I don't have to be a bus driver now. We can go and live in the beautiful countryside.' Mrs Must was surprised. 'Can we?' she asked. 'Yes! The letter is from Mr All,' Mr Must answered. 'Listen. Mr All says, "Please come and work for me at Right Farm!" Mrs Must laughed and said, 'Hurray!'

5 .... gave the letter to Mr Must.

6 Mr and Mrs Must can live in .... now.

7 .... wanted Mr Must to come and work on his farm.

8 Mr Must is happy because he can work at .... !

C Say which picture is different and why.

D Talk about how things are different now.

PROJECT

Playing and working

A ▶ **Which day did Alex do these things?**
Listen and write the day under the pictures.
Listen again and complete pictures 1 and 2.

1

.........Tuesday......... ....

2

3

....

B ▶ **Listen and draw the pictures for Thursday and Friday.**

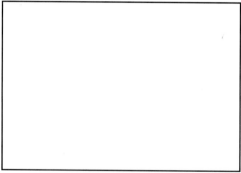

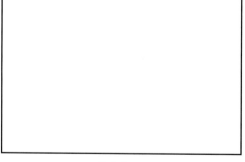

Thursday   Friday

C **Talk about the questions.**

1 Which was your best day last week? Why was it good?
2 What was the weather like last Wednesday?
3 Who did you help at home? How did you help?
4 When did you see your friends? Where did you see them?

D **Read the story. Choose a word from the box.**
Write the correct word next to numbers 1–6.

Grace works at a children's hospital which is in the city ....*centre*.......... . She's a
(1) .... Her work changes every week and sometimes, she has to work at
(2) ....

Last Tuesday, Grace slept in the day and woke up in the evening. She cooked
(3) .... and chips for her family's dinner, but Grace only wanted a cup of
coffee! After their dinner, Grace's family watched TV and then went to bed but Grace
had to get into her car and (4) .... to work.

When Grace came home on Wednesday morning, she was really tired and very
(5) .... ! She sat down at the table to have her favourite dinner – pasta!
Her children were at school and the house was quiet. Grace played some music, answered
her emails and text messages then took off her (6) .... and went to bed!

Choose the best name for this story. Tick (✔) one box.

Grace's day at work! ☐   The children's school! ☐   A new car for the family! ☐

Example				
✓ centre	sunny	nurse	fish	washed
hungry	clothes	drive	night	

E **Find the differences between the pictures.**

F **Play the game! Day words!**

39 'We've got lots of things to do'

A When do you do these things?

1 `08:00`

2 `19:30`

3 `16:00`

4 `23:00`

in the .... in the .... in the .... at ....

Do you ... write text messages?   clean your teeth?   do your homework?

When do you ... give food to your pet?   have a shower?   play outside?

B Choose the correct words and write them on the lines.

Is it **easy, difficult, boring** or **exciting** to be a farmer?

		was	is	were
Example	Farmer Jack is 90 now. He likes telling his grandchildren about when he .... *was* .... young. 'I always got up at four o'clock. I had a quick wash and a quick breakfast, then I went to see the cows in my fields.	was	is	were
1	At about seven o'clock I .... back into the house and had my second breakfast.	comes	came	come
2	I worked .... the morning, the afternoon and the evening.	on	by	in
3	When .... was something wrong with one of the animals, I sometimes had to get up	there	it	she
4	.... night and work hard then, too.	at	after	to
5	I worked .... day in all kinds of weather. I could never take a break or have a holiday but I didn't always work on Sunday evenings!'	many	every	some

C Draw lines between the question and the answer.

Do you ...

clean the bath?

cook the dinner?

wash your clothes?

make your bed?

> Oh yes! I often do that!

> I do, sometimes!

> No, never!

> Yes, every day!

> I always do that!

Do you carry .... ?   Do you work .... ?

Do you tidy .... ?   Do you paint .... ?

D ▶ Listen and write.

MILBROOK
Sports Centre

Homework

	Teacher's name:	Charlie .... Smith ....
1	Age:	....
2	Day gives tennis lessons:	on ....
3	When / Charlie's lessons:	in the ....
4	Number of children in class:	....
5	Charlie wants to teach:	.... , too.

E What about you? Complete the sentences.

1 On Monday morning, I always ....

2 In the afternoon at school, we often ....

3 In the evening, I sometimes ....

4 I never .... on Sunday night.

A Write 1, 2 or 3 words to complete the sentences about the story.

Lost in the forest!

On Sunday, Jim and Paul went to a lake with their parents. The boys and their puppy, Tiger, played on some grass next to the forest there. Paul threw a yellow ball. Tiger ran to find it in the forest, but he didn't come back again.

Examples: Jim's family went to ....*a lake*............ on Sunday.
            Tiger is the boys' ....*puppy*............ .

1   Tiger and the boys played on .... near the forest.

2   Tiger wanted to get the .... from the forest.

The boys looked for Tiger in the forest but they couldn't find him. 'We must ask someone to help us,' Jim said. 'Look! There's a police car. Quickly, Dad! Stop it!'

The car stopped and a policeman got out. 'What's the matter?' he asked. The family told him all about Tiger. 'I can help!' he said. 'Let's look by the lake again and behind the trees, too.'

3   Jim and Paul .... Tiger, but they didn't find him.

4   A .... came to help the family find their pet.

5   Everyone looked for the puppy .... and by the lake.

Paul and the policeman found something in the middle of some leaves. 'It's Tiger's yellow ball!' Paul said. And what's that noise?' Jim asked. 'Listen! By that tree? Something's black, and look, it's moving!' 'It's Tiger's tail!' laughed the policeman.

Paul ran to pick Tiger up. 'Naughty dog!' he said and laughed. Tiger jumped out of his arms and ran to the ball. 'I think he wants to play another game!' the policeman smiled. 'But I must go back to work. Have a great afternoon! And Tiger, don't get lost again!'

6   Then the policeman and .... saw Tiger's ball on the ground.

7   .... saw something black near one of the trees.

8   Paul picked Tiger up but he .... his arms.

9   Tiger wanted to play ....

10   The policeman told Tiger not to .... again!

B ▶ Listen and write.

Example	Missing pet:	PUPPY
1	When lost:	this
2	Boy's name:	Jim
3	Boy's address:	.... City Road
4	Where pet lost:	near the
5	Colour of pet:	black, white and

C Listen and say.

The boys **lookt** for their lost puppy!

D Complete the conversation about your pet.

What's the matter?

I can't find my ....

Policeman:	When did you lose your * .... ?
You:	I lost it ....

Policeman:	And what's your name?
You:	It's ....

Policeman:	Where were you when you lost your * .... ?
You:	I was ....

Policeman:	Tell me more about your * .... ?
You:	OK. It's ....

E Play the game.

F My work day!

PROJECT

41 "I had a great birthday!"

A Complete sentences about the picture. Write names and draw lines.

Lucy

1 Two people have got ....numbers.......... on their clothes.
2 The young .... who is dancing isn't wearing shoes.
3 A man with a brown .... is filming the party.
4 Above the presents, you can see three ....
5 Two of the people in the band are playing ....
6 There are some .... on the two white plates.

B Read and choose the best answer.

1 Alex: Hello Lucy! It was your birthday
          yesterday. Happy birthday!
   Lucy: A Don't worry!
          B Me too!
          C Thanks!

2 Alex: Did you enjoy your party?
   Lucy: A Yes, it was great!
          B Yes, I can come today.
          C Yes, there were two.

3 Alex: What did you do at the party?
   Lucy: A Is it a computer mouse?
          B You can make the dinner.
          C We danced and played
             games.

4 Alex: Did your mum make a cake?
   Lucy: A No, my aunt made it.
          B My mother's called Daisy.
          C Put it on the table, please.

5 Alex: How many people were at
          your party?
   Lucy: A What a nice day!
          B I don't know. Lots!
          C It was really funny!

C Read the story. Choose a word from the box.
Write the correct word next to numbers 1–6.

It was my .....birthday..... last weekend. My parents took my sister and me
to Forest Farm. Forest Farm is a kind of (1) .... where you can
see and play with lots of different animals. You can watch dogs that work
with animals like (2) .... and goats. I helped the grown-ups to
give the chickens their breakfast and my sister took a lot of photos. Then
we had (3) .... in the farm café. I had some cheese and tomato
sandwiches and Mum (4) .... my sister sausages and fries. Her
favourite! After lunch, Dad took us down to a kind of basement which
had a red door. 'Now (5) .... your eyes, Jack,' he said. I did! He
opened the door. 'You can look now' he laughed. Everyone in my class
was there! I was really (6) .... ! We played lots of funny games.
It was a great party and a very exciting day!

Example

birthday	bought	zoo
sheep	windy	close
lunch	surprised	hid

Choose the best name for the story. Tick (✔) one box.

Dad's favourite pet ☐   A great day at the farm ☐

Mum makes a cake ☐

D Find the presents and draw lines.

1   I'm pretty and you wear me round your neck.
2   I can dry you after a bath!
3   You must cook us!
4   Sit on my seat and ride me to school!
5   I'm brown and sweet to eat.

E Play the game! Birthday presents.

F Plan your party!

42 An exciting week for Jane

A **Which was Jane's best school day?**

Friday was good. It was more exciting than Thursday.

Monday was worse than Tuesday.

I enjoyed Thursday more than Tuesday.

I thought Tuesday wasn't bad ...

Wednesday was better then Friday.

My best day last week was .... because
....

My worst day last week was .... because
....

B ▶ **What did Jane do last week? Listen and draw a line from the day to the correct picture.**

Monday

Tuesday

Wednesday

Thursday

Friday

Saturday

Sunday

C **A day in the city.**

D ▶ **Charlie's going to the zoo. Listen and draw circles around his correct answers.**

Dad:	Would you like to take something to eat?	
Charlie:	Yes, please, Dad!	So do I!
Dad:	Well, here are some chicken and salad sandwiches.	
Charlie:	OK.	Excuse me!
Dad:	How about taking some orange juice, too?	
Charlie:	There they are!	Good idea!
Dad:	What about some of Grandma's coffee cake?	
Charlie:	I'm good at that.	All right!
Dad:	And would you like to buy an ice cream at the zoo?	
Charlie:	How are you?	No, thanks!
Dad:	And have you got your ticket, Charlie?	
Charlie:	Yes. Don't worry!	I think it is.

E **Find the differences between the pictures.**

F **Play the game! Say thanks.**

43 'My holidays'

A Let's talk about holidays.

1 Do you enjoy going on holiday?
2 What do you like eating on holiday?
3 Who do you go on holiday with?
4 What do you like doing on holiday?

a My grandparents.
b Yes, it's great.
c At the beach.
d Playing tennis.
e Coffee ice cream.

Tell me about your last holiday.

B Read and choose the best answer.

1 Mr Ride: Did you enjoy your holiday, Jill?
  Jill: A Last year.
     B All right!
     C Yes, thanks!

2 Mr Ride: Where did you go?
  Jill: A We sat in a circle.
     B To the jungle.
     C On Monday afternoon.

3 Mr Ride: How did you get there?
  Jill: A Bring your bike!
     B I'm crossing the road.
     C We went by helicopter.

4 Mr Ride: What sport did you do on your holiday?
  Jill: A We went swimming.
     B You did that on Friday.
     C Someone played it.

5 Jill: Here are two photos!
  Mr Ride: A No, I'm frightened!
     B Wow! They're great!
     C Excuse me, Jill!

C Find the differences between the pictures.

D Read Fred's story. Write the correct word next to the numbers.

My holiday by Fred Top

My name's Fred and I (Example) ....*love*....... going on holiday. For our holiday last year, we went to an island. I enjoyed being there a lot. We travelled there by (1) .... That was exciting too! It was hot and (2) .... every day on the island, but at night it sometimes rained and rained.

The food there was great. We often ate (3) .... and Dad cooked fish on the beach one day too! Everyone went swimming in the morning and then we went for long walks every afternoon. I took my (4) .... with me because I wanted to take lots of photos of everything that I saw there. I brought some really pretty shells home. I gave the best one to my (5) .... She really loved it.

sunny   ~~love~~   camera   plane
clever   pineapples   climb   grandma

E Complete sentences about two dream holidays!

mine   yours

	mine	yours
I'd love to go to	....	....
I'd love to travel there by	....	....
I'd love to go there with	....	....
On my dream holiday, I'd love to	.... and and .... !	.... and and .... !

F Answer questions! What an exciting trip!

G An island project.

PROJECT

44 On the sand and by the sea

A **Look at the pictures. Tell the story.**

1  2  3  4

B **Complete the sentences about the story. Write 1, 2 or 3 words.**

The wet T-shirts!

Last Tuesday, Sam and his brother Nick went to the beach. They put their towels and clothes down on the sand and played football. Then they ran and jumped into the water.

Example Nick has a ......*brother*...... called Sam.

1 Before their swim, the boys had a game of ....

2 After their game, the boys .... into the sea.

The boys swam under the water to look for shells and sea animals. Then they swam back up again and climbed on to some rocks. They sat there and watched the sailing boats, then Nick saw something orange in the water by their feet. He picked it up and said, 'Look! It's your orange T-shirt, Sam! You put it too near to the sea!'

3 Nick and Sam looked for sea animals and .... in the water.

4 Then the boys sat on a rock to watch ....

5 Nick saw Sam's .... in the sea.

Then Nick saw his green T-shirt in the sea, too and said, 'Quick, Sam! Get it for me!'

The brothers swam back to the beach with their wet T-shirts. When they got there, only one of their shoes was on the sand. 'We put those too near the sea, too,' Sam said.

They walked to the bus stop in their wet clothes and then caught a bus home. When they told their parents about their day. Mum said, 'You must be more careful!' 'But we're happy that you're both safe!' Dad added.

6 The boys lost three of their .... in the water.

7 Nick and Sam stood by a .... to wait for their bus.

8 Their parents were happy because the boys were ....

C Read the sentences and find the answers in the story.

1 After a swim, you can dry your body with these. ....*towels*....................
2 T-shirts, trousers and skirts are examples of these. ....
3 This is under your feet when you walk on a beach. ....
4 You can climb up or on to these. They're often grey. ....
5 You need a ticket to travel on this in town. a ....
6 These people are your mother and your father. ....

D Read the sentences. Write words which mean the same.

1 take something off the floor   p_ _ _ something u_
2 have a swim   g_ f_ _ a swim
3 take a bus   c_ _ _ _ a bus
4 go for a walk   h_ _ _ a walk
5 put on your clothes   g_ _ d_ _ _ _ _ _
6 go to the shops   g_ s_ _ _ _ _ _ _

E Find ten more pairs! Draw lines.

write   I   pair   read   son   aunt

wear   red   sun   for   eye   where

eight   know   sea   see   no   right

aren't   four   ate   pear

F Find the differences between the pictures.

1

2

G Play the game! Let's find A–Z.

45 'Treasure!'

A Look and read. Choose the correct words and write them on the lines.

a ticket   coconut   maps   treasure

trees   islands   a pirate   a boat

Example

This person is in stories and sometimes he has a parrot!   *a pirate*

1 You have to buy this when you go to watch a film.   ....

2 When it's cold, the leaves on these sometimes fall to the ground.   ....

3 You look at these to find roads to different towns.   ....

4 These places have water all round them.   ....

5 Pirates look for this under the water or under the ground.   ....

6 You sit in this to go sailing or fishing in the sea.   ....

B Colour the words you can make from the name of the film!

Pirates and Parrots

| tests | parents | sports | seats | trousers | parties | sisters | dinner | pandas |

C Write 1, 2 or 3 words to complete the sentences about the film.

Last week, my parents and I read about a film on the internet. We bought the tickets and went to see it at the *Star Cinema* on Sunday. The film was about a famous pirate called Dan. He had a black beard and moustache and was very strong. He had a parrot whose name was Clever. Clever always sat on Dan's shoulder.

Examples The boy and his _____parents_____ read about the film on the internet.
On Sunday, they went to see the film at _the Star Cinema_ .

1 There was _____ in the film whose name was Dan.

2 Dan the pirate was really _____ !

3 Clever was Dan's _____ .

In the film, Dan and his pirates sailed to a small island. When they got to the beach, Dan was hot and tired. 'Go and find something to eat!' he said to the pirates. 'Something for Clever too!' Dan's pirates climbed trees and found some bananas, pineapples and coconuts to eat. They sat down in a circle on the sand, ate and then slept after all their work.

4 The pirates went by boat to a _____ .

5 Dan was _____ when he sat down on the sand.

6 Dan told the pirates to _____ everyone some food.

7 The pirates all had something to eat, then they
_____ on the beach.

Then Clever made a really loud noise and Dan and the pirates woke up. Clever jumped up and down and said, 'Pretty treasure! Pretty treasure!' 'Clever's never wrong. There's treasure here!' Dan said. The pirates found the box under the sand and laughed very loudly when they looked inside. That night, they sang and danced and played music on the sand. I loved the film. It was great!

8 Dan knew that there was some _____ under the sand because Clever was always right!

9 When the pirates saw the treasure in the box, they _____ .

10 The pirates played some _____ and sang and danced on the beach.

D Talk about differences between pictures 2 and 3.

E Lets write five-line poems!

How many people and how many names can you see?

(A) ▶ **Listen and draw lines.**

Sam   Peter   Vicky   Grace

Sally   Alex   Jack

(B) **Look and read. Write yes or no.**

Examples

The boy in the big boat has a black hat on his head.   ...yes....

One of the children is swimming in the sea.   ....no....

Questions

1   The woman in the pink dress is wearing a pair of glasses.   ....

2   Everyone on this beach is sitting on the sand.   ....

3   There's a picture on the sail of the bigger boat.   ....

4   Two birds are sitting on the top of the tree.   ....

5   You can see a parrot inside the boy's cage.   ....

6   Only one person is trying to catch a fish.   ....

(C) **Listen and say.**

The **pirate** in the **big boat** has a **black hat** on his **head!**

D Say which picture is different and why.

E Listen, write the words, questions and answers.

?

?

?

?

F Write your question and yes or no answer.

Question .... ?

Answer: ....

G Play the game! Guess my question.

47 The different things we do

A Things I do. Draw lines.

1 answer   **a**   my best coat
2 wait at   **b**   my phone
3 invite   **c**   up in funny clothes
4 put on   **d**   a train
5 catch   **e**   all my homework
6 dress   **f**   my friends to a party
7 laugh   **g**   the bus stop
8 do   **h**   at funny films

B Listen and tick (✔) the box.

1 What's Peter doing now?

A ☐   B ☐   C ☐

2 What's Jane doing now?

A ☐   B ☐   C ☐

3 What's Paul doing now?

A ☐   B ☐   C ☐

4 What's Alex doing now?

A ☐   B ☐   C ☐

C Draw a circle round the word that means the same thing!

lift   eara__he   elevator   everyone

shop   store   sp__rt   skate

film   moon   moustac__e   movie

football   son   __occer   soup

sweets   candy   centre   c__untry

flat   a__phabet   armchair   apartment

Now make a word with the missing letters! ....

....

garden

....

E **Who is doing what? Write names and complete the sentences.**

1 .... and ....   are w........................ !
2 ....   is s........................ on a seat.
3 ....   is j........................ into the water.
4 ....   is w........................ a T-shirt.
5 ....   is s........................ in the pool.

F **Say 'Yes, that's right' or 'No that's wrong'!**

G **Play a game! Change places or Mime the words!**

48 We want to do this one day

A What are your answers? One day, would you like to ... ?

1

2

3

4

5

6

7

8

B Read and choose the best answer.

Example

Tom: Hello, Jane. What are you reading?

Jane: A   Upstairs in my bedroom.

   B   A book about a boy and his boat.

   C   I can't this afternoon.

Questions

1   Tom: What did the boy do?

   Jane: A   He sailed round the world.

      B   That's his funny story!

      C   He's not by the beach.

2   Tom: Who gave you the book?

   Jane: A   No, it's my sister's.

      B   Is it hers or his?

      C   My Dad bought it.

3   Tom: Do you like the book?

   Jane: A   Yes, you are.

      B   Yes, it is.

      C   Yes, I do.

4   Tom: Is it a very long book?

   Jane: A   There aren't many pages.

      B   I'm sorry about that.

      C   Her hair's really long.

5   Tom: Can I read it after you?

   Jane: A   Don't worry!

      B   Yes, OK!

      C   So do I!

C **Read the story. Choose a word from the box. Write the correct word next to numbers 1–6.**

Last Tuesday, Jane's father bought his daughter a ..... *present* ..... from the new bookshop in the town centre. It was a story that Jane wanted to read about a (1) .... who sailed round the world in a very small boat. Her name was Mary Banks and she was only 22. It was a very exciting story. Mary saw (2) .... and sharks in the sea. She was often (3) .... but she was never frightenend. When Mary came home, lots of people wanted to read about her.

There was a website about Mary's trip round the world and a story about her on the back (4) .... of one of Jane's comics! Jane loved reading about Mary. 'Can we (5) .... a boat, Dad?' she asked. 'I want to sail round the world, too!' Jane's father smiled. 'I think that's a great idea, Jane. But first you must learn to (6) ....!'

Example

present   tired   downstairs

woman   buy   whales

swim   page   raining

Choose the best name for the story. Tick (✔) one box.

Dad's new boat ☐

Learning about Mary ☐

Jane's sailing lesson ☐

D **Write a story about a story! Choose words.**

E **Let's see! How well do you know your friend?**

49 'Ask me another question'

A **Make sentences with these words.**

1   **Miss Page:**   this? / What's

               What's this?

2   **Sam:**   don't / I / Sorry, / know

          ....

     Miss Page: It's a helicopter.

3   **Sam:**   please? / again / you / Can / say / that

          ....

     Miss Page: It's a helicopter.

4   **Sam:**   do / How / spell / you / helicopter ?

          ....

     Miss Page: H–E–L–I–C–O–P–T–E–R.

     Sam: H–E–L–I–C–O–P–T–E–R. OK! Thank you.

B **Talk about the picture.**

C Where are these things things in the picture? Draw lines.

The coat is	in the cupboard.
The fan is	between the coat and the fan.
The rainbow is	on the handbag.
The helicopter is	above the sea.
The mouse is	behind the woman's head.
The dolphin is	below the clock.
The map of the world is	next to the window.

D Answer questions and draw pictures.

What was the weather like yesterday?
It was ....

What's the weather like today?
It's .... and ....

What's the teacher's school bag like?
It's .... and it's got a
.... on it.

What's your school bag like?
It's .... and it's got
....

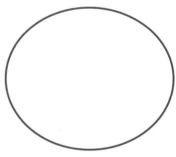

E Read and choose the best answer.

Example

Mrs Pat: Hello, Sue.
Sue: A Good morning!
        B Thank you!
        C Well done!

1 Mrs Pat: How old are you, Sue?
    Sue: A Fine, thanks.
          B I'm ten.
          C Sue Young.

2 Mrs Pat: Who do you play with?
    Sue: A In the playground.
          B At the end of school.
          C My friends.

3 Mrs Pat: What sports do you play?
    Sue: A My football's at home.
          B Baseball and tennis.
          C Mum or sometimes, Dad.

4 Mrs Pat: What's your classroom like?
    Sue: A It's mine.
          B Class six.
          C It's really nice.

5 Mrs Pat: When do you do your homework?
    Sue: A In the evening.
          B At the library.
          C Very clever.

F Choose answers and questions!

G Listen and answer!

A   Say what you see in the pictures.
Find words that sound the same.

B   ▶   Listen and tick (✔) the box.

Example: Which is Daisy?

A ☐   B ☐   C ☐

1   What does Kim need?

A ☐   B ☐   C ☐

2   Where is Tony now?

A ☐   B ☐   C ☐

3   What is on Ben's computer screen?

A ☐   B ☐   C ☐

4   What did Pat do in his test?

A ☐   B ☐   C ☐

5   What does Jim want to do now?

A ☐   B ☐   C ☐

C Play the game! Stepping stones.

the end

z you see animals here

y not today

5 things you can see in the country

v smaller than a town

w not better

u not downstairs

t not bottom

4 places in a town

s not weak

r not square

q not loud

p children play here

3 places with water

o not closed

n not good

k a room in a house

l not first

m you climb this

j another place with trees

i not outside

h not cold

g not terrible

f a place with trees

e not boring

d not clean

c not straight

b not ugly

a not before

the start

2   Animals, animals ...

1   Crocodiles eat fish, birds, animals and sometimes they eat people too! They do not eat grass or plants.
2   A crocodile has a long body and mouth and a long tail. A crocodile has short legs. But be careful because they can swim and they can run too!
3   A mother crocodile sits on her eggs for about 12 weeks then the eggs open. The mother carries her baby crocodiles into the river.
4   You can find crocodiles in many parts of the world. Some crocodiles only live in rivers but some crocodiles can live in the sea too.
5   When crocodiles swim they can see. Their mouths are under the water but their eyes are above the water. A crocodile's eyes are on the top of its head.
6   Look inside a crocodile's mouth and you can find a lot of teeth! They can have between 60 and 80 teeth. People have about 30 teeth.
7   Crocodiles are dangerous animals. You should never go near them!

5   The woman in the red dress

Learner A
Let's talk about the clothes you wear.
1   What clothes would you like to buy?
2   What do you wear when it's wet?
3   What **don't** you wear when it's cold?
4   What do you wear at home?
5   Where do you put your clothes at night?

9   Me and my family

Learner A
Now let's talk about you and your family.
1   How many people are there in your family?
2   Does your family live in a house or in a flat?
3   What do you do with your family at weekends?
4   Tell me about the youngest person in your family.

26 Guess who lives here?

11 Things we eat and drink

Learner A

Let's talk about you and food.

1 Who buys your food?
2 Where does your family buy their food?
3 What do you have for breakfast?
4 What vegetables do you like?
5 What's the name of your favourite place to eat?

Now find words inside the words!

meat

sandwich

orange

5   The woman in the red dress

Learner B
Let's talk about the clothes you wear.
1   Where do you get dressed?
2   What colour are your favourite clothes?
3   What clothes are you wearing now?
4   What clothes **don't** you wear when it's hot?
5   What's the **last thing** you put on in the morning?

9   Me and my family

Learner B
Now let's talk about you and your family.
1   How many cousins have you got?
2   Does your family live by the sea or in a town?
3   Where do you go with your family on holiday?
4   Tell me about the oldest person in your family.

11   Things we eat and drink

Learner B
Let's talk about you and food.
1   Who cooks the meals in your house?
2   Where do you have lunch?
3   Do you help in the kitchen at home?
4   What fruit don't you like?
5   What food is your country famous for?

Now find words inside the words!
mango
carrot
candy

20 Where?

Learner A: Colour the biggest mountain blue, the boy's hair brown, the girl's bag pink, the trees on the left green, the rock behind the boy grey.

21 Here and there in town

Learner A
Let's talk about your town.
Where do you like going on Saturdays?
What do you do there?
Who do you go there with?
Tell me about your favourite place in town.

20   Where?

Learner B: Colour the boy's bag purple, the girl's jacket yellow, the smallest duck on the right orange, the trees on the right red.

21   Here and there in town

Learner B

Let's talk about your town.

Where does your family buy your food?

How do you go there?

When do you go there?

Tell me about your favourite place in town.

27 Seeing differences

Talk about these questions:

1 Do you like hopping games? Why/why not?
2 Do children at your school skip in the playground? What's your favourite playground game? How do you play it?
3 What games do you play when you're home? Who do you play with?
4 What kind of weather is good for skating? Have you got a pair of skates at home?
5 Does anyone that you know have to wear a hat at work? What's their job? Why do they have to wear a hat?

28   Our busy holidays

37   Mr Must changes his job

Learner A

When I was a bus driver ...
I had to .... a uniform.
I .... to say 'Good morning' to everyone who got on my bus.
I had to .... the dirty bus.
I couldn't .... in bed because I had to get up!
I couldn't have any pets because we .... in a small flat.

38   Playing and working

Learner A
Ben's week

	Monday	Tuesday	Wednesday	Thursday	Friday
Morning					
Afternoon					
Evening					

43   My holidays

Answer questions.

What an exciting trip!

When did you go on your trip?

....

Where did you go?

....

Who did you go there with?

....

How did you get there?

....

What did you do first when you got there?

....

Which part of the trip was really exciting?

....

Would you like to go on a trip like this again?

....

37   Mr Must changes his job

Learner B

Now, because I work on a farm
I can't stay in bed but I like getting up because I .... my job!
I have to .... the farm truck when it's dirty.
I can .... lots of pets!
I can .... the clothes that I like!
I can .... 'Hello' to the farm animals!

38   Playing and working

Learner B
Anna's week

	Monday	Tuesday	Wednesday	Thursday	Friday
Morning					
Afternoon					
Evening					

40   People who help us

This driver lives in
....

This driver gets up at .... o'clock.

This driver has .... for breakfast.

This driver takes a .... with them to work.

This driver drives to .... at eleven o'clock.

At one o'clock, this driver stops work and walks to the
....

This driver phones their ....

This driver has .... for lunch.

This driver starts work again at ....

There are lots of .... in this driver's lorry /
truck / bus.

Sometimes, this driver has to drive to ....

At five o'clock, this driver is ....

This driver goes home and
....

This driver really
.... their job!

Unit wordlist

1

places
playground

verbs
climb
dance
hop
jump
kick
move
run
skate
skip
talk
walk
watch

adjectives
good at

adverbs
all day
round

2
animals
baby
bat
bear
bird
cage
cat
cow
crocodile
dog
dolphin
fish
fly
frog

goat
kangaroo
lion
lizard
monkey
mouse/mice
panda
parrot
penguin
rabbit
shark
tail
whale
zoo

verbs
sound like
prepositions
about (12 weeks)

3
animals
chicken
duck
kitten
pet
puppy
sheep

places
farm
field

verbs
be called
help
would like

adjectives
frightened of
sweet

4
body and face
beard
eye
face
hair
moustache

people
alien
film star

other nouns
line

colours
black
blue
brown
gray
green
grey
orange
purple
red
white

verbs
change
look in the mirror
paint

adjectives
blonde
curly
fair
long
short
straight
ugly

5
clothes
coat
dress
hat
jacket
jeans
pair
scarf
shirt
shoe
skirt
sock
sweater
trousers
T-shirt

things
bag
glasses

verbs
carry
get dressed
put on
wear

prepositions
behind
into
next to

6
body and face
arm
back
ear
foot
hand
head
leg

mouth
neck
nose
shoulder
stomach
tooth/teeth

sports and leisure
monster
player
robot

animals
wing

verbs
go home
hold

7
weather
cloud
rain
rainbow
snow
weather
wind

the world around us
moon
star
sun

leisure
painting
painting class

verbs
draw
fly a kite
get wet
rain
snow

adjectives
cloudy
cold
double
hot
sunny
windy

expressions
Oh dear!
Well done!
Wow!

8
animals
elephant
fur
giraffe
polar bear

weather
kind of weather

the world around us
part of the world

verbs
get cold
go to bed
sleep
wake up

adjectives
clever
dry
strong
tall
wet

adverbs
today
yesterday

9
family
aunt
brother
cousin

dad
daughter
father
grandchildren
granddaughter
grandfather
grandma
grandpa
grandparents
grandson
mother
mum
parent
sister
son
uncle

verbs
answer
ask
call (name)
make a noise

adjectives
busy
loud
old
quiet
young

expressions
Good idea!

10
people
sports teacher

daily life
phone number

verbs
cook
give music lessons
invite
stop
wait
wash

adjectives
nice

expressions
Here you are.
So do I.

11
fruit
apple
banana
coconut
fruit
grape
lemon
lime
mango
orange
pear
pineapple
watermelon

meat
burger
chicken
sausage

vegetables
bean
carrot
onion
pea
potato

drinks
coffee
drink
juice
lemonade
milk
tea
water

food
bread
candy
cheese

chips
chocolate
egg
fish
fries
ice cream
pasta
rice
salad
sandwich
soup
sugar
sweet

verbs
grow
make
plant

12
food and drink
bottle
bowl
box
cup
glass
plate

birthday
balloon
birthday
party
present

the home
CD player
cupboard
shelf
table

sport
baseball
bat

verbs
add

adjectives
big
round
square

adverbs
inside
outside

13
the home
balcony
basement
bookcase
chimney
flower
front door
garden
grass
hall
home
leaf
mat
roof
stairs
wall
window

leisure
cameraman
film
movie
video

verbs
have a wash

adjectives
closed
exciting
famous
open

adverbs
downstairs
upstairs

prepositions
above
below
in front of
inside
on
outside

expressions
Come on!
How exciting!
Really?

14
the home
address
apartment
bathroom
bedroom
dining room
flat
ground floor
house
kitchen
lift
living room
room

shapes
circle
pentagon
rectangle
square
triangle

adjectives
dark
light

adverbs
downstairs
upstairs

prepositions
near

15
leisure
guitar
music
piano

school
answer
board
classroom
computer mouse
cross
desk
homework
keyboard
lesson
listening
map
page
pencil
picture
question
reading
rubber
ruler
speaking
test
tick
writing

verbs
make a mistake
play music
point
talk

adjectives
correct
right
wrong

16
sports and leisure
badminton
ball game
basketball

fishing
football
game
hockey
horse riding
ice skating
player
sailing
skating
soccer
sports centre
table tennis
tennis
TV

verbs
hit
kick
laugh
play (football)
shout
swim
throw
watch

adjectives
boring
favourite
fun
funny
great
OK

expressions
Help!

17
sports and leisure
comic
comic book
dancing
drawing
DVD
DVD player
hobby

radio
story
swimming

beach
beach
rock
sand
sea
towel

verbs
bounce
enjoy
like
love
wave

18
health
doctor
hospital
nurse
temperature

places
seat

work
driver

verbs
have a temperature
take your
temperature

adjectives
bad
careful
hungry
terrible
tired
well

pronouns
where
who
that

19
health
backache
cold
cough
dentist
earache
headache
stomach-ache
toothache

people
boy
girl
man
woman

verbs
hurt

adjectives
all right
fine

expressions
Don't worry
What's the matter?

20
places
bank
market
supermarket

food and drink
picnic

other nouns
noise

verbs
buy
get better
go for a bike ride
have a picnic

adjectives
afraid
thirsty

21
places
café
cinema
library
park
station
sweet shop
town

the home
chair

animals
tiger

transport
postcard
ticket

clothes
handbag

verbs
catch a bus
choose
go for a swim
have a drink
have lunch
see a doctor

adverbs
here
there

questions
what
where
who

expressions
Hi
I've got to go!
See you!

119

22

places
bookshop
bus stop
city
road
shopping centre
shop window
street
village

numbers
hundred
thousand

verbs
go for a boat ride
know
think

23
**the world
around us**
country
country(side)
forest
island
jungle
lake
mountain
river
waterfall
world

animals
snake

adjectives
high

prepositions
down
up

determiners
many

conjunctions
because
or

questions
How much?

24
technology
email
(the) internet
message
photo
text
video
website

school
alphabet
letter

other nouns
difference

verbs
add photos
call
get a message
make a video
phone
take pictures
text

adverbs
only

pronouns
everyone
some

25
the home
armchair
fan
sofa
toothbrush

animals
hippo

verbs
cry
learn
ride a horse
say yes
want

adjectives
beautiful
different
pretty
small
ugly

adverbs
well

conjunctions
but

expressions
sorry

26
the home
CD
lamp

animals
snail
spider

verbs
come home
drive to work
move into a flat

prepositions
after
before
between
from
opposite
out of
round

**prepositional
phrases**
at home
at the back of
at the bottom of
at the end
at the top of
on top of

27
leisure
band

work
at work
job

other nouns
idea

verbs
find
go for a walk
have a dream
put
run a lot
see
watch a video
write a song

adjectives
asleep
naughty

28
people
best friend
wife

transport
a balloon ride
helicopter

time
school holiday

verbs
fish
go running
go sailing
go shopping
go swimming
hide
make a cake

adverbs
always
never
often

determiner
every

questions
How often

29
toys
doll

verbs
clean your teeth
drop
fall asleep
learn English
wave goodbye

adjectives
surprised

adverbs
badly
carefully
loudly
quickly
quietly
sadly
slowly
very
well

30
people
grown-up

school
art
marks
maths
spelling

verbs
go away on holiday
Let's talk
listen to music
sing songs
test
use a keyboard

questions
How?
How many?
How old?
When?
Which?
Why?

expressions
bye
goodbye

31
the home
bath
blanket
shower

animals
snail
zebra

toys
teddy bear

verbs
cry
have a shower
need

adjectives
angry
clean
dirty
happy
new
sad

determiner
another

32
food
kilo
tomato

verbs
understand

adjectives
angry
empty
safe

adverbs
first
then

prepositions
behind

pronouns
everything
nothing

determiners
all
a little
a lot of
not many
not much
some

expressions
Thank you
try looking

33
time
Friday
Monday
Saturday
Sunday
Thursday
Tuesday
Wednesday
watch
week
weekend

places
pool
swimming pool

verbs
give someone a
present

adjectives
last

34
transport
kilometre

work
clown

places
circus

verbs
colour a picture
dress up
find
give someone a
present
open a present
plant
put on
show
start to rain
stop playing
talk about

adverbs
now

35
school
school things

transport
bus stop
place

food
breakfast
dinner
lunch
supper

time
diary

verbs
get off the bus
get on the bus
get to school
get up
wake up

adjectives
late

adverbs
late

36
animals
panda

school
pen

verbs
clean
could
do your homework
fall out of your bag
invite someone for dinner
lose

questions
Whose?

37
transport
motorbike
truck

places
bus station
town centre

work
bus driver
uniform

home
CD
clock
toy

verbs
drive a bus
dry
get undressed
have to
smile
start the bus
stay in bed

expressions
Good morning
Hello
Hurray!

38
time
afternoon
day
evening
morning
night

places
children's hospital
city centre

verbs
answer emails
take off (clothes)

39
people
age
name

verbs
cook the dinner
give food to a pet
have a holiday
have a quick breakfast
have a quick wash
make your bed
take a break
teach
tell someone about
work hard
write a text message

adjectives
easy
something wrong

adverbs
sometimes

40
transport
lorry
truck

work
driver
police car
policeman

verbs
come back
get lost
look for
lose
must

adjectives
missing

adverbs
again

determiners
another

pronouns
someone
something

questions
What's the matter?

41
verbs
close
film
play the piano

pronouns
lots

expressions
Excuse me
Happy birthday!
How about …?
Me too!
What about …?
No, thanks.
OK.
Thank you.
Yes, please.

42
verbs
make friends with
take someone on a trip

adjectives
best
better
more exciting
worse
worst

expressions
all right

43
transport

camera
dream holiday
plane

**the world
around us**
shell

time
last year

verbs
bring
cross the road
go on holiday
sit in a circle
travel

44
animals
sea animals

travel
sailing boat

other nouns
example

verbs
get undressed
have a swim
mean the same
pick up
take a bus
wait for a bus

prepositions
by the sea

exclamations
Be careful!
Quick!

45
other nouns
pirate
treasure

verbs
buy a ticket
climb trees
fall
go fishing
have something to
eat

adjectives
awake
crazy
scary

pronouns
whose

46
transport
sail

clothes
a pair of glasses

verbs
catch a fish
dress up like a pirate
read about
swim in the sea

47
places
elevator
store

school
eraser

verbs
catch a train
drive a sports car
invite someone to a
party

play garden games
laugh at funny films
travel to the moon
wait at the bus stop

48
verbs
make friends with
an alien
learn about
learn to swim
read e-books
read stories
ride on an elephant
sail round the world
go and see your
grandparents
walk under a
waterfall
would like

49
home
clock

verbs
spell

expressions
Can you say that
again?
How do you
spell …?
I don't know.
Sorry
What's … like?

50
school
English test
listening test
spelling test

leisure
football game
screen

adjectives
difficult
easy

Irregular verbs

Verb	Past simple	Translation
be	was/were	....
bring	brought	....
buy	bought	....
can	could	....
catch	caught	....
choose	chose	....
come	came	....
do	did	....
draw	drew	....
dream	dreamed/dreamt	....
drink	drank	....
drive	drove	....
eat	ate	....
fall	fell	....
find	found	....
fly	flew	....
get	got	....
give	gave	....
go	went	....
have	had	....
hide	hid	....
hit	hit	....
hold	held	....
hurt	hurt	....
know	knew	....

Verb	Past simple	Translation
learn	learned/learnt	....
lose	lost	....
make	made	....
mean	meant	....
put	put	....
read	read	....
ride	rode	....
run	ran	....
say	said	....
see	saw	....
sing	sang	....
sit	sat	....
sleep	slept	....
spell	spelled/spelt	....
stand	stood	....
swim	swam	....
take	took	....
tell	told	....
think	thought	....
throw	threw	....
understand	understood	....
wake up	woke up	....
wear	wore	....
write	wrote	....